Focus on Canada

Population Dynamics in Canada

By: **Don Kerr**
       Bali Ram

Catalogue No. 96-305E

Published by Statistics Canada and Prentice Hall Canada Inc.

PRENTICE HALL

Statistics   Statistique
Canada   Canada

Canadä

Canadian Cataloguing in Publication Data

Kerr, Don
Population Dynamics in Canada

(Focus on Canada series)
CS96-305E
Issued also in French under the title:
La dynamique de la population au Canada.

1. Demographic transition -- Canada.
2. Population geography. 3. Age -- Canada -- Statistics.
4. Sex -- Statistics. 5. Marriage -- Canada -- Statistics.
6. Canada -- Demographics -- Statistics.
7. Canada -- Census, 1991.
I. Ram, Bali. II. Statistics Canada. III. Title.
IV. Series: Focus on Canada (Ottawa, Ontario).

HA741.5. 1991k 304.6'0971'021 C94-931063-8

Published by authority of the Minister
responsible for Statistics Canada

© Minister of Industry,
Science and Technology, 1994

ISBN 0-13-150830-X
Published by Statistics Canada and Prentice Hall Canada Inc.

Acquisitions Editor: Michael Bickerstaff, Prentice Hall Canada Inc.
Product Manager: Lorna Bailie, Statistics Canada

1 2 3 4 5   98 97 96 95 94

Printed and bound in Canada.

Distributed by: Prentice Hall Canada Inc.
                   1870 Birchmount Rd.
                   Scarborough, Ontario
                   M1P 2J7

Preface

Focus on Canada is a series of publications portraying the people of Canada. The portrait is drawn through the analysis of the data collected by the 1991 Census of Population and Housing. Each publication examines a specific issue and provides a demographic, social, cultural and economic perspective.

The authors of this series have taken special care to make their analysis informative and easy to read. They make use of descriptive graphs and data tables to more clearly illustrate the information. Often the results are compared to previous censuses, showing how Canada and Canadians have changed over time.

The publications were prepared by analysts at Statistics Canada, and reviewed by peers from within the Agency as well as experts from external organizations. I would like to extend my thanks to all the contributors for their role in producing this useful and interesting publication.

I would like to express my appreciation to the millions of Canadians who completed their questionnaires on June 4, 1991. Statistics Canada is very pleased to be able to now provide this summary of the results. I hope you enjoy reading this study -- and the others in this series.

Ivan P. Fellegi
Chief Statistician of Canada

Contents

Contents (continued)

List of Tables

List of Charts

Contents (concluded)

List of Appendix Tables

Highlights

- Since 1951-56, the rate of population growth in Canada has declined, reaching an all-time low of 4.0% during 1981-86. The trend was reversed during 1986-91 when Canada's population increased by 7.9%.

- Over the 1986-91 period, British Columbia retained its status as Canada's fastest growing province, exhibiting a population increase of 13.8%, whereas Saskatchewan experienced a loss of 2.0%.

- Between 1986 and 1991, Oshawa was the fastest growing Census Metropolitan Area (18%), followed by Vancouver (16.1%), and Kitchener (14.5%) while Thunder Bay (1.8%) and Chicoutimi-Jonquière (1.6%) were the slowest growing.

- In 1971, the 5.4 million persons aged 25 to 44 made up a quarter of Canada's population. With the influx of the baby boom generation (1946-66), this age group increased to include 9.2 million persons in 1991, forming a third of the total population.

- Canada's population of high school age (14 to 17 years) has steadily declined since 1976, from 8.3% to 5.5% in 1991.

- Canadian society is aging rapidly. The number of persons 65 years and over grew by 128% between 1961 and 1991 -- from 1.4 million to 3.2 million. The number of persons 75 years and over grew by 154% to 1.3 million during the same period.

- There are far more women then men among seniors. In 1961, there were 94 elderly men (65 years and over) for every 100 elderly women. By 1986, this ratio had dropped to 72 per 100 and has remained virtually unchanged since then.

- Among seniors (65 years and over), the ratio of widows to widowers has been increasing steadily; the ratio was three to one in 1961 compared to five to one in 1991.

- More Canadians are delaying marriage. In 1991, 30% of women aged 25 to 29 had never been married, compared with only 15% in 1971. During the same period, the percentage of never-married women in the 30 to 34 age group increased from 9% to 16%.

- The number of Canadians living common-law grew from about 713,000 in 1981, to 974,000 in 1986. In 1991, it reached 1,452,000.

Introduction

Demographic change can have immediate social and economic consequences for society as a whole, or for specific sectors and institutions within society. It has a direct bearing on, for example, the size and vitality of the labour force, and the demand for housing, education and health services. The present study highlights some of the most fundamental demographic changes that have influenced the well-being of Canadians over recent years.

There are many changes of a demographic nature that have had a major imprint on the character of Canadian society. For example, Canada's baby boom generation (born between 1946 and 1966) is gradually making its way into its middle years, to be replaced by smaller age groups born during Canada's baby bust (young adults and children born during the 1970's and 1980's). Accordingly, a smaller proportion of Canadians are presently experiencing childhood than ever before in the history of this country. The purpose of the present study is to document population dynamics in the Canadian context, using information from Canada's National Censuses up to 1991.

Chapter 1 covers the distribution and growth of Canada's population across space and time. This is a key topic in a country long noted for its regionalism. Chapter 2 examines the age structure of Canada's population. Since social relationships within societies are influenced by the relative size of specific age groups, of interest are Canadians of school, working, and retirement age. Chapter 3 explores the sex structure of Canada's population. While at first glance, it is obvious that roughly equal numbers of males and females coexist in Canada, among the elderly this balance does not hold. Chapter 4 highlights the marital characteristics of Canada's population. Although differences occur across regions of the country, Canadians are now more likely than in the past to live in a common-law union, marry at a later age, and experience separation or divorce. The study concludes with a brief overview of Canada's demographic patterns.

Chapter

1

Population Growth and Distribution

In 1991, Canada's population was 27.3 million. This is more than five times what it was at the turn of the century and almost twice as large as when Newfoundland joined Confederation in 1949. As a result of the baby boom and relatively high levels of immigration, Canada's population grew rapidly from the end of World War II until the 1970s. Over more recent decades, the pace of growth has noticeably slowed, a direct result of a declining birth rate.

Chart 1.1
Population Growth, Canada, 1956-1991

Millions

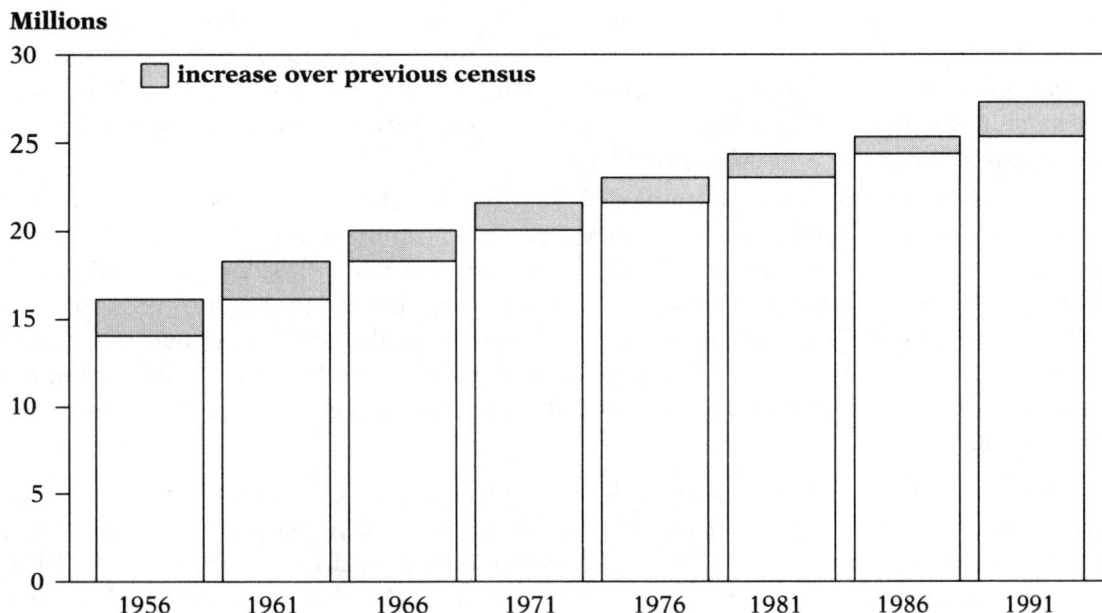

Source: Statistics Canada, *Age, Sex and Marital Status*. 1991 Census of Canada, Catalogue No. 93-310, Table 1.

As **Chart 1.1** shows, Canada's population increased very quickly during 1951-1956, climbing 14.8%. Growth slowed gradually to an all-time low from 1981 to 1986 of only 4%, a very low rate by both historical and international standards.

In the most recent intercensal period (1986 to 1991), there was a departure from this long-term trend. Canada's rate of population growth actually rebounded somewhat, with an increase of 7.9%. Several factors explain this change, including a significant growth in immigration to Canada, a slight decline in emigration from Canada, a modest upturn in the number of births, and the inclusion for the first time of non-permanent residents in the 1991 Census (e.g., foreign students, workers and refugees).

Immigration was the most important factor. The number of immigrants to Canada increased steadily in the late 1980s. With respect to non-permanent residents, the 1991 Census shows that about 1% of Canada's population fall within this category. If non-permanent residents are excluded from the 1991 census count, the estimated increase during 1986-1991 is slightly below 7%.

Growth Patterns Across Canada's Provinces and Territories

Canada's population growth has varied considerably over time, and across provinces and territories. Certain regions have consistently grown faster than the national average, while others have invariably fallen behind. For example, as **Chart 1.2** shows, from 1951 to 1991, the two territories, British Columbia, Alberta, and to a lesser extent, Ontario, have all grown faster than the national average. On the other hand, Quebec, Manitoba, Saskatchewan and the Atlantic provinces have all grown slower, partly because of out-migration of persons to other provinces.

Over the most recent intercensal period, 1986 to 1991, British Columbia has retained its status as Canada's fastest growing province. British Columbia's increase was 13.8% -- a net growth of almost 400,000 persons **(Table 1.1).** Only the Yukon had a more rapid rate of population growth, although this has a very small impact on national figures because of its relatively small population. Ontario, Canada's most populous province, had the second highest provincial increase at 10.8% -- almost one million people. At the other end of the spectrum, Saskatchewan had a net loss of 2.0%, the only province to lose population over this period.

Growing at a pace comparable to the nation as a whole, Alberta ranked third among provinces in population growth from 1986 to 1991 with a 7.6% increase. This was not nearly as high as its rate during the 1970s -- its population increased 21.7% from 1976 to 1981. Quebec, on the other hand, with an increase in 1986-1991 that ranks fourth among provinces, not only grew more rapidly than in the previous intercensal period, but also had its highest rate since the early 1960s. Quebec gained 350,000 persons (5.6%), reversing a long-term decline in its growth rate, which reached an all time low during 1981-1986.

Chart 1.2
Percentage Growth, Canada, Provinces and Territories, 1951-1991

Percentage Growth

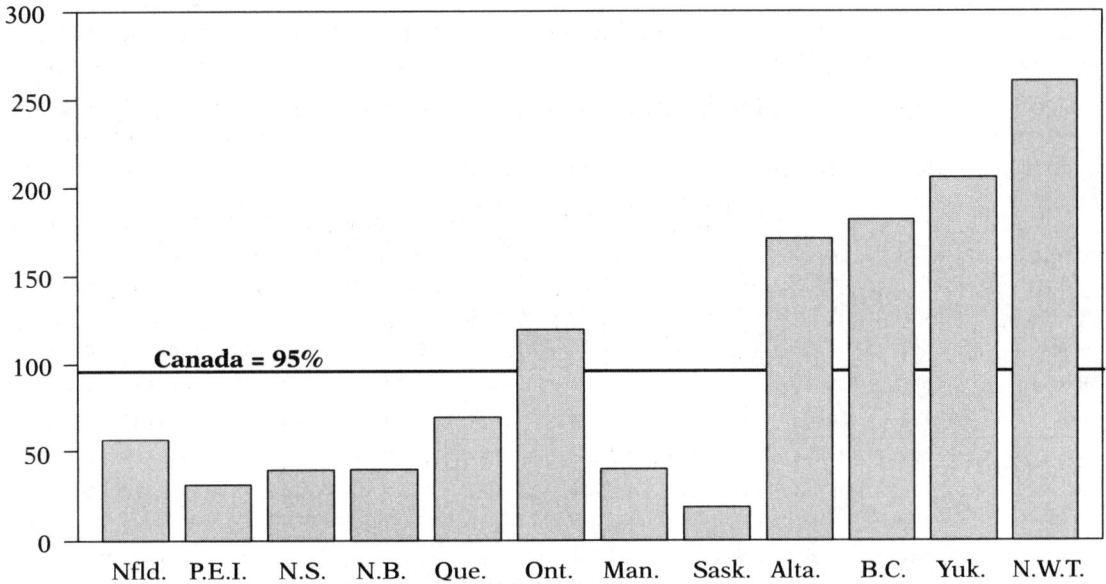

Source: Statistics Canada, *Age, Sex and Marital Status.* 1991 Census of Canada,
Catalogue No. 93-310, Table 1.

With the exception of the Northwest Territories, the rest of the country grew more slowly than the national average during 1986-1991. For example, Manitoba's population increased by fewer than 30,000 (2.7%) over this 5 year period. With respect to the Atlantic provinces, the size of Newfoundland's population remained virtually unchanged, Nova Scotia experienced an increase of only 3.1%, while Prince Edward Island and New Brunswick retained low growth of 2.5% and 2.0% respectively. In Canada's slowest growing provinces, higher than average rates of out-migration and lower than average ability to attract immigrants explain the low rates.

Expanding Cities

Canada's population is becoming increasingly metropolitan. Metropolitan Canada has grown at a faster rate than has the country as a whole, although many cities are exceptions to this rule. For many decades, internal migration and international immigration have brought people to Canada's larger cities.

Table 1.1
Population Growth, Canada, Provinces and Territories, 1951-1991

Population

Province/Territory	1951	1956	1961	1966	1971	1976	1981	1986	1991
Canada	14,009,429	16,080,791	18,238,247	20,014,880	21,568,310	22,992,600	24,343,180	25,309,330	27,296,855
Nfld.	361,416	415,074	457,853	493,396	522,105	557,725	567,680	568,350	568,475
P.E.I.	98,429	99,285	104,629	108,535	111,640	118,230	122,510	126,645	129,765
N.S.	642,584	694,717	737,007	756,039	788,960	828,570	847,445	873,180	899,945
N.B.	515,697	554,616	597,936	616,788	634,560	677,250	696,405	709,445	723,900
Quebec	4,055,681	4,628,378	5,259,211	5,780,845	6,027,765	6,234,445	6,438,400	6,532,460	6,895,960
Ontario	4,597,542	5,404,933	6,236,092	6,960,870	7,703,105	8,264,465	8,625,110	9,101,695	10,084,885
Manitoba	776,541	850,040	921,686	963,066	988,250	1,021,505	1,026,245	1,063,015	1,091,940
Sask.	831,728	880,665	925,181	955,344	926,245	921,325	968,310	1,009,615	988,930
Alberta	939,501	1,123,116	1,331,944	1,463,203	1,627,875	1,838,040	2,237,725	2,365,825	2,545,550
B.C.	1,165,210	1,398,464	1,629,082	1,873,674	2,184,620	2,466,605	2,744,470	2,883,370	3,282,065
Yukon	9,096	12,190	14,628	14,382	18,390	21,835	23,150	23,505	27,795
N.W.T.	16,004	19,313	22,998	28,738	34,805	42,610	45,740	52,240	57,650

Percentage change

	1951-1956	1956-1961	1961-1966	1966-1971	1971-1976	1976-1981	1981-1986	1986-1991
Canada	14.8	13.4	9.7	7.8	6.6	5.9	4.0	7.9
Nfld.	14.8	10.3	7.8	5.8	6.8	1.8	0.1	0.0
P.E.I.	0.9	5.4	3.7	2.9	5.9	3.6	3.4	2.5
N.S.	8.1	6.1	2.6	4.4	5.0	2.3	3.0	3.1
N.B.	7.5	7.8	3.2	2.9	6.7	2.8	1.9	2.0
Quebec	14.1	13.6	9.9	4.3	3.4	3.3	1.5	5.6
Ontario	17.6	15.4	11.6	10.7	7.3	4.4	5.5	10.8
Manitoba	9.5	8.4	4.5	2.6	3.4	0.5	3.6	2.7
Sask.	5.9	5.1	3.3	-3.0	-0.5	5.1	4.3	-2.0
Alberta	19.5	18.6	9.9	11.3	12.9	21.7	5.7	7.6
B.C.	20.0	16.5	15.0	16.6	12.9	11.3	5.1	13.8
Yukon	34.0	20.0	-1.7	27.9	18.7	6.0	1.5	18.3
N.W.T.	20.7	19.1	25.0	21.1	22.4	7.3	14.2	10.4

Source: Statistics Canada, *Age, Sex and Marital Status*. 1991 Census of Canada,
Catalogue No. 93-310, Table 1.

A majority of Canadians now live in metropolitan areas with a population of at least 100,000 **(Table 1.2).** The 1991 Census found 6 out of every 10 Canadians in one of Canada's 25 census metropolitan areas (CMAs). As an example of the pace at which metropolitan Canada's population has expanded, 76.4% of the country's total population growth during 1986-1991 occurred within CMAs, which together grew by 10.0%, or 1.5 million persons.

As an urban way of life has become a reality for most Canadians, some provinces have witnessed faster metropolitan growth than others. For example, as **Chart 1.3** illustrates, the fastest growing CMAs during 1986-1991 tended to be in either Ontario or British Columbia -- 7 of the 8 metropolitan areas that grew at a faster pace than the CMA average are in these provinces. Most immigrants and interprovincial migrants settle in CMAs.

During 1986-1991, Oshawa was the fastest growing CMA in Canada, followed by Vancouver, Kitchener, Toronto and Victoria. Calgary was the only CMA outside of Ontario and British Columbia to grow faster than the CMA average. Chicoutimi/Jonquière, Thunder Bay, Saint John, Windsor, and Regina had the lowest growth rates. All CMAs grew, but the range in growth rates was wide.

Over the years, this variation has had important ramifications for the relative size of metropolitan areas. For example, until 1976, Montreal was Canada's largest CMA; it was in that year surpassed by Toronto (which has grown at a much quicker pace ever since). Similarly, Winnipeg, historically the gateway to Canada's west, ranked fourth among CMAs in 1961, but dropped to seventh place by 1991. On the other hand, other western cities such as Edmonton and Calgary climbed rapidly in ranking (particularly during the economic prosperity associated with the oil boom of the 1970s). Ottawa-Hull also grew quickly to become Canada's fourth largest CMA, while Vancouver maintained third place with very high levels of growth. Interestingly, Halifax, the largest CMA in Atlantic Canada, has ranked thirteenth overall since 1951.

Future trends in Canada's population growth and distribution will likely raise many economic, social and policy issues. For example, the fastest growing CMAs are also the most prosperous. What are the long-term implications of this fact? Should present immigration levels be maintained? What is relatively certain is that if Canada had no immigration, growth would be very low. This is due to Canada's fertility rate, which has been below replacement for over two decades.

Table 1.2
Population of Census Metropolitan Areas[1], 1986 and 1991

Census Metropolitan Areas	Population in 1986	Population in 1991	Percentage Increase
All CMA's	15,148,055	16,665,350	10.0
Toronto	3,431,720	3,893,045	13.4
Montreal	2,921,355	3,127,240	7.0
Vancouver	1,380,730	1,602,500	16.1
Ottawa–Hull	819,260	920,855	12.4
Edmonton	773,880	839,920	8.5
Calgary	671,325	754,030	12.3
Winnipeg	625,305	652,355	4.3
Quebec	603,270	645,550	7.0
Hamilton	557,030	599,760	7.7
London	342,305	381,525	11.5
St. Catharines–Niagara	343,255	364,550	6.2
Kitchener	311,195	356,420	14.5
Halifax	295,990	320,500	8.3
Victoria	255,145	287,900	12.8
Windsor	253,990	262,075	3.2
Oshawa	203,540	240,105	18.0
Saskatoon	200,665	210,025	4.7
Regina	186,520	191,695	2.8
St. John's	161,900	171,855	6.1
Chicoutimi–Jonquière	158,465	160,930	1.6
Sudbury	148,880	157,610	5.9
Sherbrooke	129,960	139,195	7.1
Trois–Rivières	128,885	136,300	5.8
Saint John	121,265	124,980	3.1
Thunder Bay	122,220	124,430	1.8

[1] According to 1991 boundaries.

Source: Statistics Canada, *Age, Sex and Marital Status.* 1991 Census of Canada, Catalogue No. 93–310, Table 3.

Chart 1.3
Population Growth for Census Metropolitan Areas[1], 1986-1991

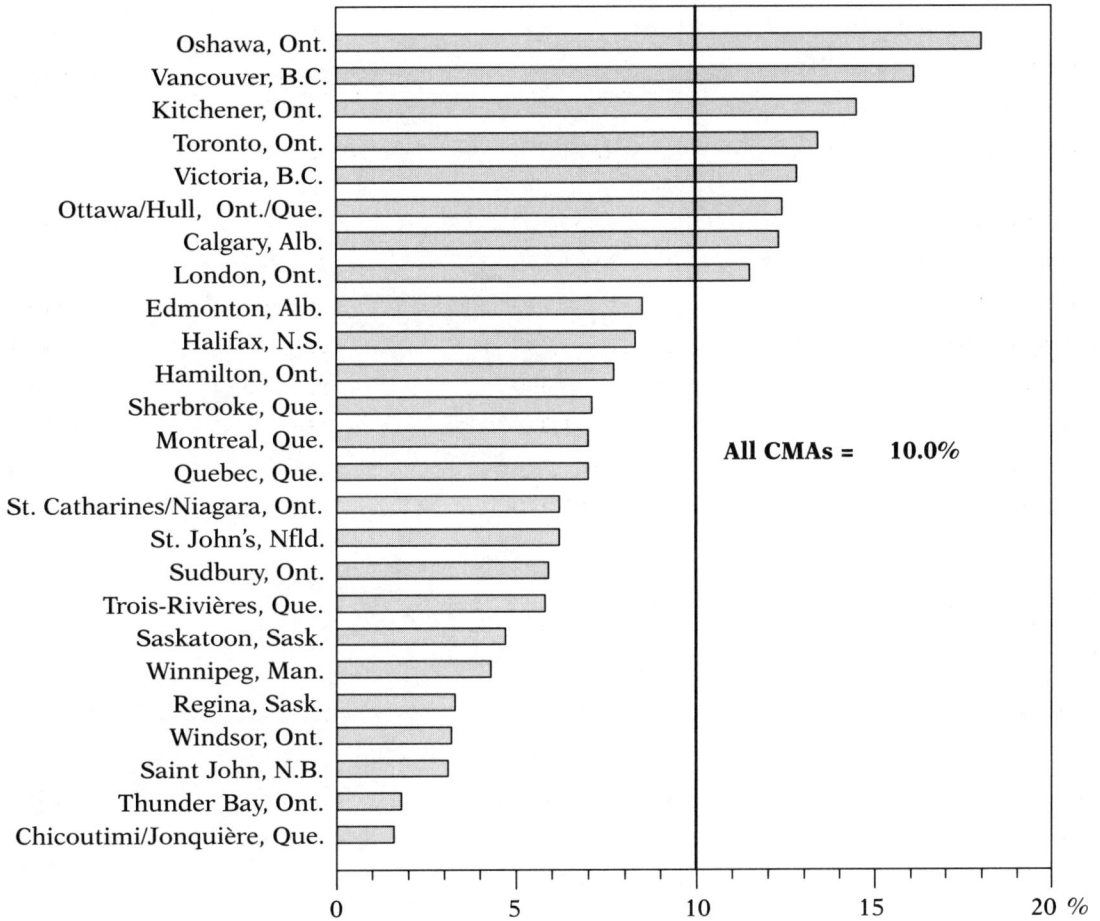

Oshawa, Ont.	
Vancouver, B.C.	
Kitchener, Ont.	
Toronto, Ont.	
Victoria, B.C.	
Ottawa/Hull, Ont./Que.	
Calgary, Alb.	
London, Ont.	
Edmonton, Alb.	
Halifax, N.S.	
Hamilton, Ont.	
Sherbrooke, Que.	
Montreal, Que.	
Quebec, Que.	
St. Catharines/Niagara, Ont.	
St. John's, Nfld.	
Sudbury, Ont.	
Trois-Rivières, Que.	
Saskatoon, Sask.	
Winnipeg, Man.	
Regina, Sask.	
Windsor, Ont.	
Saint John, N.B.	
Thunder Bay, Ont.	
Chicoutimi/Jonquière, Que.	

All CMAs = 10.0%

(x-axis: 0, 5, 10, 15, 20 %)

[1] According to 1991 boundaries.

Source: Statistics Canada, *Age, Sex and Marital Status*. 1991 Census of Canada, Catalogue No. 93-310, Table 3.

Chapter

2

Age Structure

In recent decades, Canada's age structure has changed in many important ways. The ability of Canadians to adapt to these changes is key to continued social and economic well-being. Many of our services and institutions are closely tied to specific age groups, including day-care, educational services, the housing industry, health care, pension plans, and institutional support for seniors.

Changes in Canada's Age Structure

Population pyramids are useful for summarizing how Canada's population is distributed by age and sex. The pyramids for 1961, 1971, 1981 and 1991 in **Chart 2.1** demonstrate that Canada's population has moved from a broad-based pyramid (with a large proportion of the population at younger ages) to one with a contracted base and an expanded centre (with a larger proportion in the middle years).

Three fundamental components of demographic change can influence the age structure of a population: births, deaths and migration. In Canada, the birth rate continues to be of particular consequence. The number of births in Canada has fluctuated substantially in recent decades, with immediate ramifications for the country's age structure. The birth rate was relatively low in the 1930s, climbing significantly during the baby boom (1946-1966), only to fall to an unprecedented low in the late 1960s and 1970s (Canada's "baby bust").

The low birth rate that characterized the 1930s is perhaps most clearly reflected in the 1961 age distribution, with the population pyramid somewhat pinched about ages 20 to 24. If we follow this same age group (birth cohort) through to the 1991 Census, the 1991 distribution is correspondingly pinched at about ages 50 to 54. The high birth rate of the baby boom is evident in the broad base of the 1961 pyramid, while the expanded middle of the 1991 pyramid shows this same group thirty years later. The baby bust is best reflected in the relatively constricted base of the 1991 pyramid. Overall, these fluctuations have produced a population pyramid in 1991 that is atypical by historical standards.

Chart 2.1
Population by Age and Sex, Canada, 1961, 1971, 1981 and 1991

1961

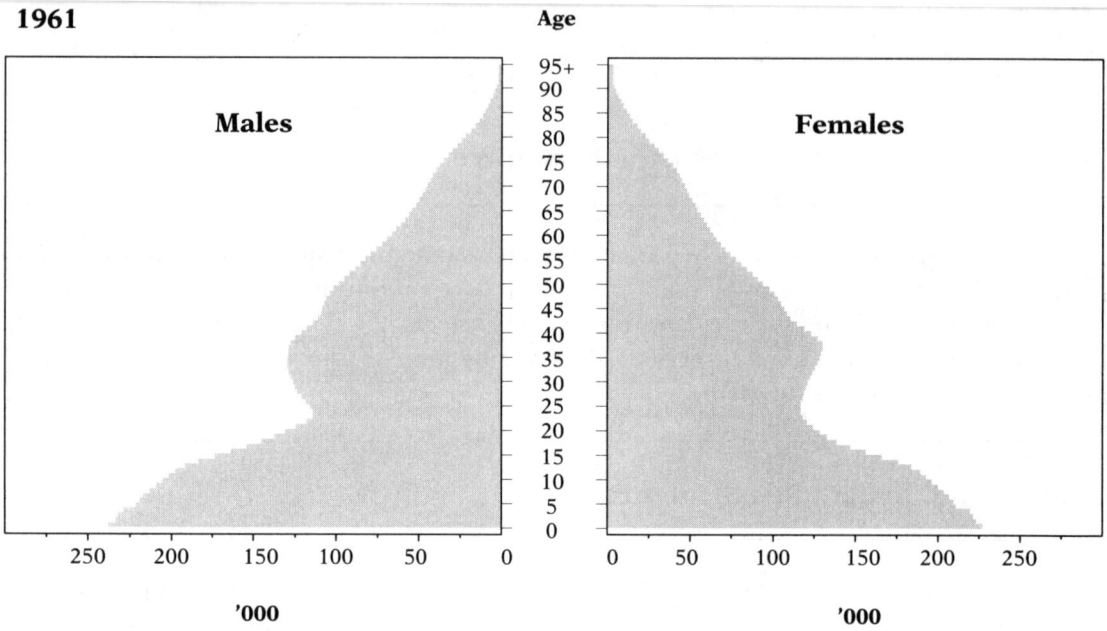

1971

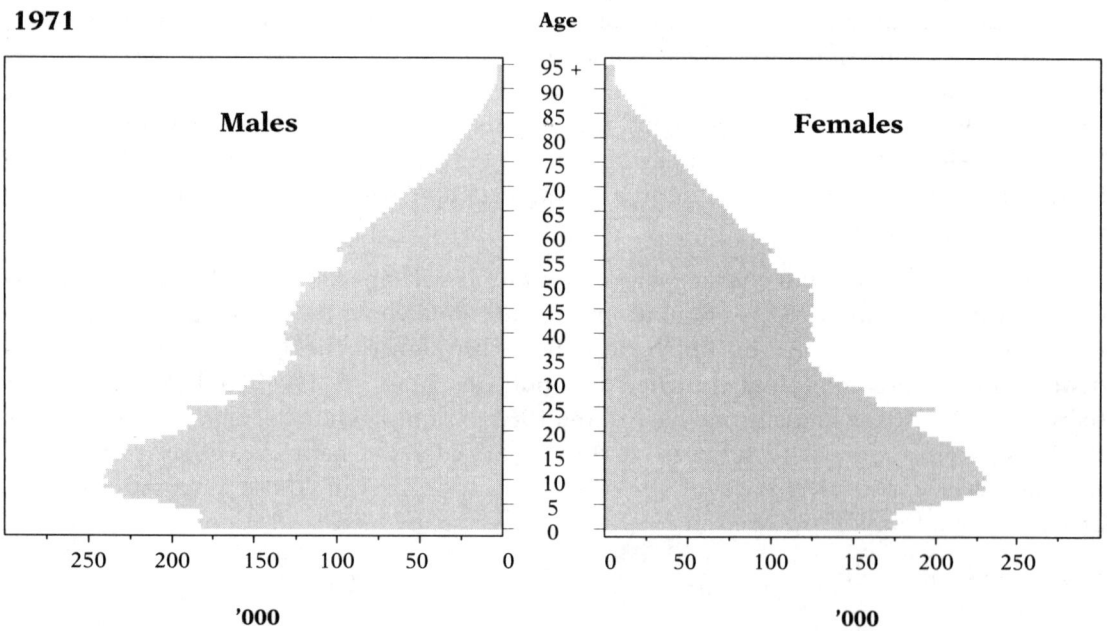

1981

Age

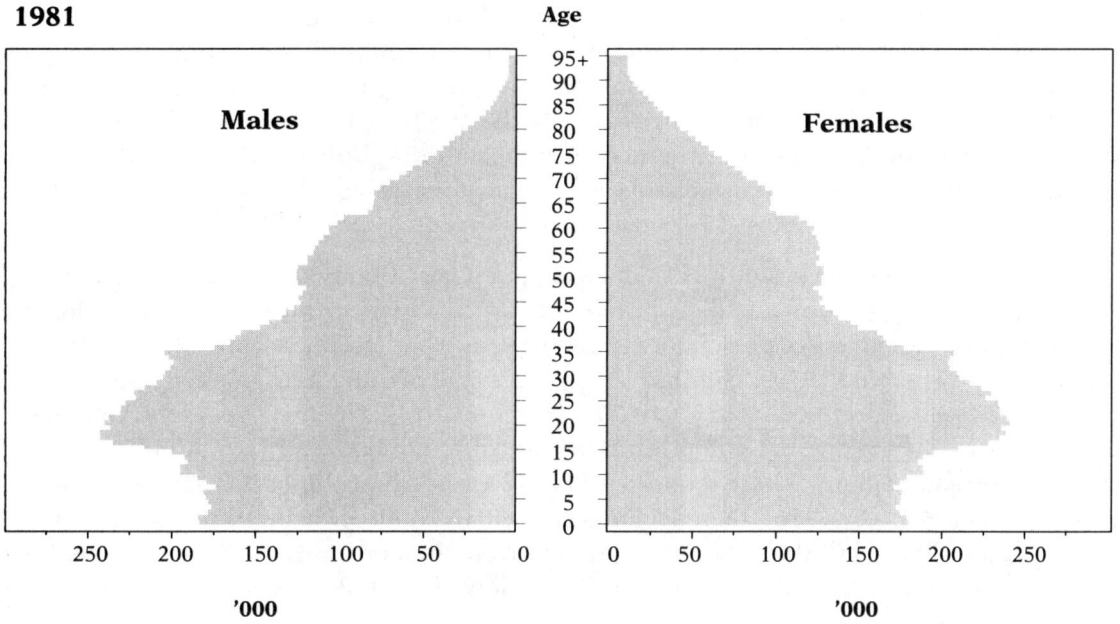

95+
90
85
80
75
70
65
60
55
50
45
40
35
30
25
20
15
10
5
0

Males

Females

250   200   150   100   50   0   0   50   100   150   200   250

'000   '000

1991

Age

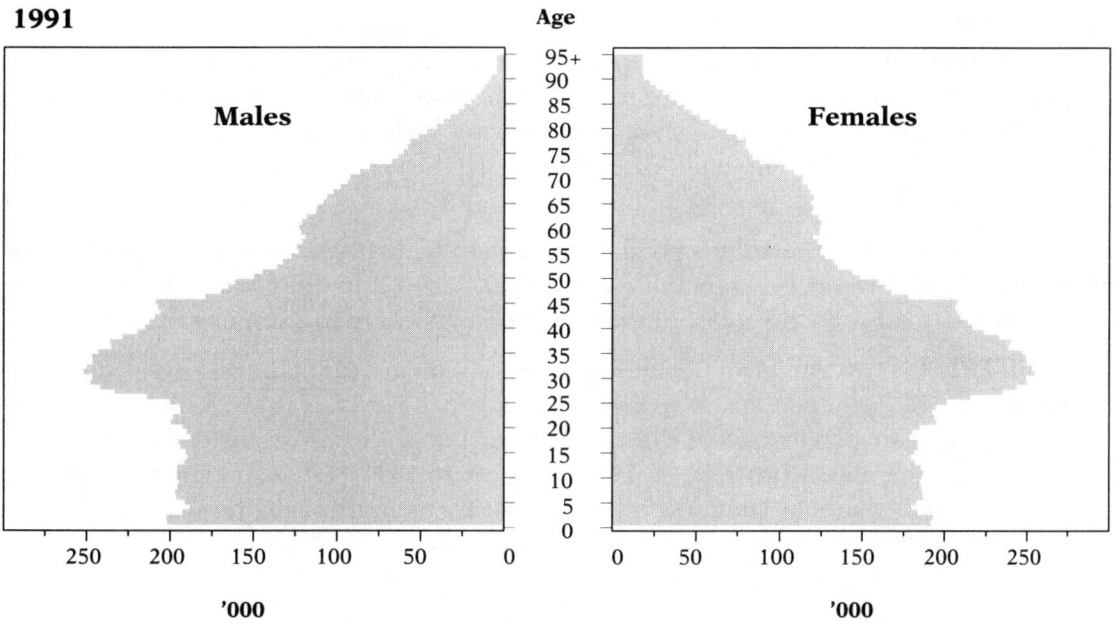

95+
90
85
80
75
70
65
60
55
50
45
40
35
30
25
20
15
10
5
0

Males

Females

250   200   150   100   50   0   0   50   100   150   200   250

'000   '000

Source: Appendix Table A.1

The baby boom has prompted substantial change in many institutions because of its size compared to the birth cohorts that predated and followed it. Consequently, the baby boomers have always attracted considerable attention from demographers and non-demographers alike. This was true during the 1960s and 1970s when they induced a rapid expansion of Canada's educational system. As these large birth cohorts moved through Canada's primary and secondary schools, administrators struggled to develop new facilities and hire more teachers.

This shift in the age structure of the Canadian population is also evident in **Chart 2.2,** which shows the percentage distribution of selected age groups. For example, the percentage of Canadians of preschool age (0 to 4 years) had dropped from 12.4% in 1961 to about 7.5% by the mid 1970s. Similarly, the percentage of Canadians of elementary school age (5 to 13 years) declined from about 19.7% in 1961 to 12.5% in 1991. As the large birth cohorts born during the baby boom moved out of childhood and into adolescence, the percentage of Canadians of high school age (14 to 17 years) first climbed (from about 6.8% in 1961 to about 8.3% by 1976), then declined steadily to about 5.5% by 1991. Since the birth cohorts that followed the baby boomers are relatively smaller, many of the societal changes that accommodated the baby boom have either slowed, curtailed, or actually reversed.

As the baby boomers made their way into young adulthood, expansion in Canada's school system was replaced by a rapid increase in the number of Canadians seeking employment. The percentage of Canadians in their younger working years (ages 18 to 44) rose steadily from the early 1970s onward, from about 37.6% in 1971 to 43.8% by 1991. Canada's baby boomers have only recently moved into their middle years -- typically the most productive in terms of labour force involvement. The smaller number of children born during the baby bust are just beginning to take on the responsibilities of young adults. While the baby boomers are experiencing some of their most demanding years in terms of the labour market, family life and child care, those born during this country's baby bust have only most recently moved into their early twenties.

The percentage of Canadians potentially in their later years of employment (45 to 64 years) has also increased, from about 17.4% in 1961 to 19.7% by 1991. This older age group will continue to grow as the oldest of the baby boomers begin to swell its ranks.

Similarly, the percentage of Canadians at retirement age (65 years and over) will climb as Canada's age pyramid becomes increasingly top heavy. Already, Canada's seniors comprise a greater percentage of the population than ever before in our history. This percentage has climbed from 7.6% in 1961 to 11.6% in 1991. Life experience rather than youthfulness will characterize Canada's age structure as it gradually moves into the 21st century.

Chart 2.2
Population by Selected Age Groups, Canada, 1961-1991

Percentage

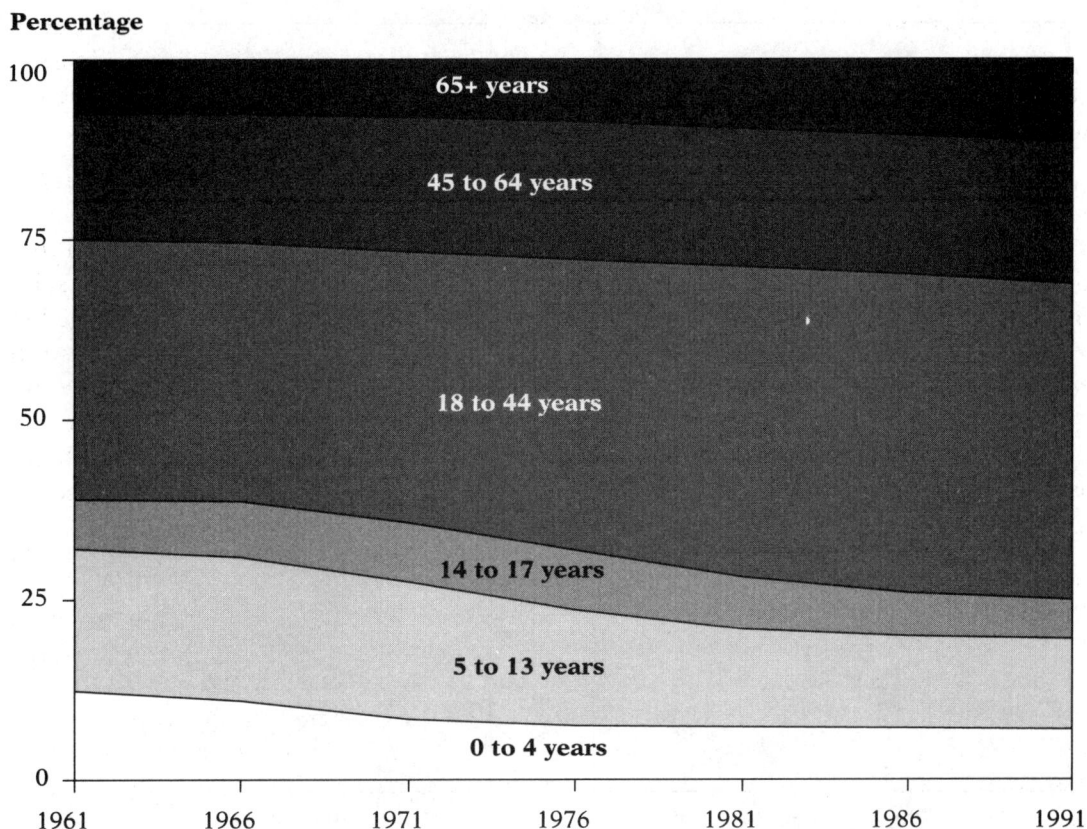

Source: Appendix Table A.1

In the most recent intercensal period 1986 to 1991, the baby boom bulge continued to be felt. **Chart 2.3** superimposes the 1986 and 1991 population pyramids. As the bulge moves up Canada's age structure, the number of Canadians in later adolescence and early adulthood has noticeably declined. For example, the 1986 pyramid was particularly wide for the 20 to 24 age group; by 1991 this segment of the pyramid had narrowed considerably. In contrast, for immediately older age groups, the pyramid segments have widened.

The most pronounced change from 1986 to 1991 occurred for the 40 to 44 age group, which grew by 29.2%, from 1.6 to 2.1 million. Some age groups shrank, particularly the 20 to 24 year group, down by 12.9% from 2.2 to 2.0 million. Overall, the relative proportion of Canadians under 30 years of age continued to decline, while the number in their middle years grew. The number of Canadians of retirement age also increased by 17.5% from 2.7 to 3.2 million.

Chart 2.3
Population by Age and Sex, Canada, 1986 and 1991

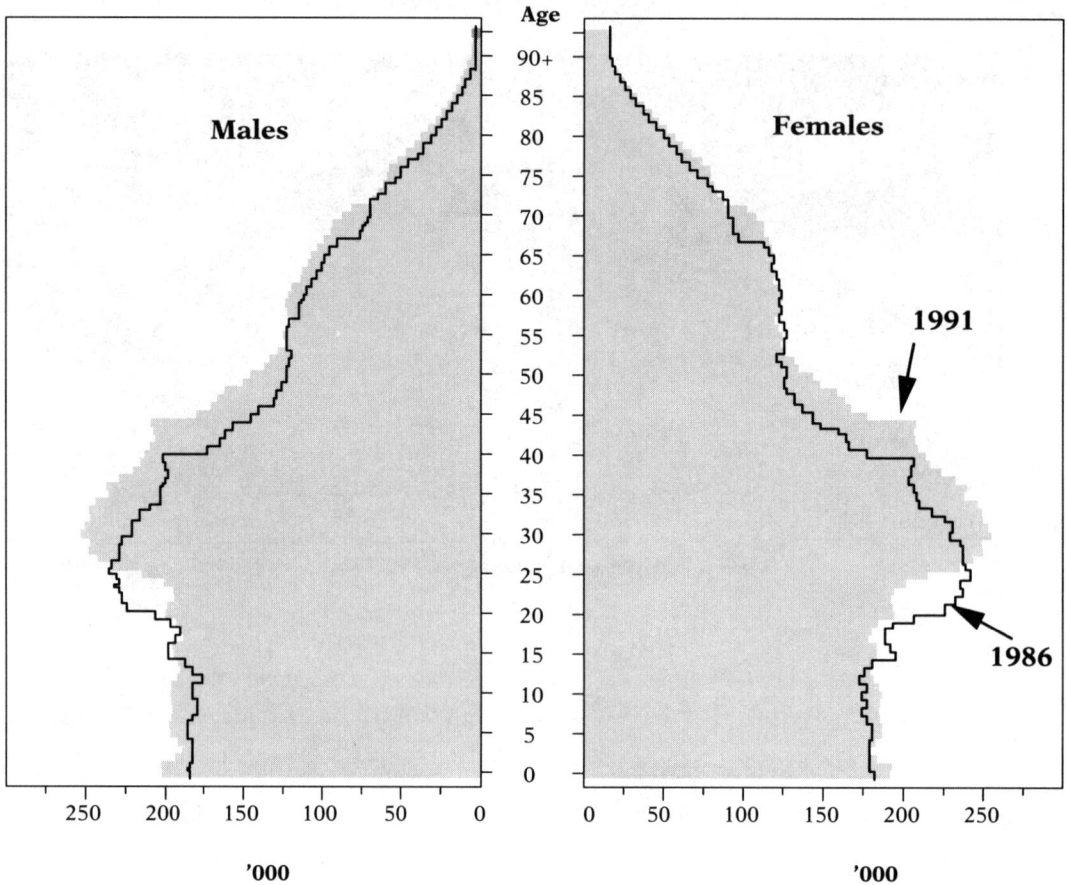

Source: Appendix Table A.1

An Aging Population

One of the most notable demographic trends in Canada is the aging of the population. In 1961, Canada's population included a large proportion of children and a relatively small number of seniors; by 1991 the pyramid had an expanded centre and a growing proportion in their retirement years. This shift will likely continue for many decades, particularly as the large baby boom cohorts make their way into their senior years.

This is reflected in how the median age of Canadians has increased -- the point in the age distribution whereby half of the population is older and the other half is younger **(Table 2.1).**

In 1961, the median age was about 26.3 years; in 1991, it was 33.5 years, an increase of 7.2 years over three decades.

Table 2.1
Median Age, Canada, 1961-1991

Year	Median age
1961	26.3
1966	25.4
1971	26.3
1976	27.8
1981	29.6
1986	31.6
1991	33.5

Source: Appendix Table A.3

Although all components of demographic change -- births, deaths and migration -- can influence the aging process, the fact that Canadians are having fewer children today relative to the past continues to be of particular consequence. The total fertility rate in Canada has for many years been below the replacement level (2.1 births for each woman during her reproductive years) and continues to be the single most important factor in explaining why Canada's population is aging. Fertility always has an impact on the same segment of the age pyramid (i.e. the bottom), while the effect of mortality and migration is felt across all ages. While a reduction in the birth rate inevitably leads to fewer infants and a reduced proportion at younger ages, change in other demographic factors is more subtle, and depends upon which age groups are affected (e.g., whether a prospective immigrant is young or old, whether the relative risk of death is reduced at younger or older ages, and so on).

This is exemplified by the effect of mortality upon Canada's age distribution. Although there have been some significant reductions in mortality and improvements in the life expectancy of Canadians, until recently, this trend influenced the aging process marginally. Before 1971, these gains did not contribute noticeably to the aging process because they occurred primarily as a consequence of reductions in infant mortality. Only more recently has this situation changed, with a greater proportion of older Canadians living well into their senior years.

As with mortality, the effect of international migration is spread across a wide variety of ages. Both the young and old immigrate to and emigrate from Canada. As well, because the birth rate for immigrants is not significantly higher than among Canadians in general, increased immigration has not significantly increased the relative proportion of children in Canada's population.

Changes in Canada's Dependent Population: Children and Seniors

As a result of population aging, there have been important changes in the relative number of Canada's two major dependent populations, children and seniors. To examine these changes, demographers often refer to the age dependency ratio (defined as the ratio of the number of persons in economically dependent parts of the population to the number in economically productive parts). This generally means comparing the number of children (0 to 17 years) and seniors (65+) to the number of persons of working age (18 to 64 years). This index is usually expressed as the number of children and elderly per 100 population of working age.

Overall, the age dependency ratio in Canada declined substantially from 1961 to 1991 **(Chart 2.4).** In 1961, the ratio was 87 dependants per 100 persons of working age; by 1991, it had declined to about 58 per 100. It is often argued that a relatively low dependency ratio lessens the costs borne by the working population, and thus helps a society achieve affluence.

Chart 2.4
Age Dependency Ratios, Canada, 1961-1991

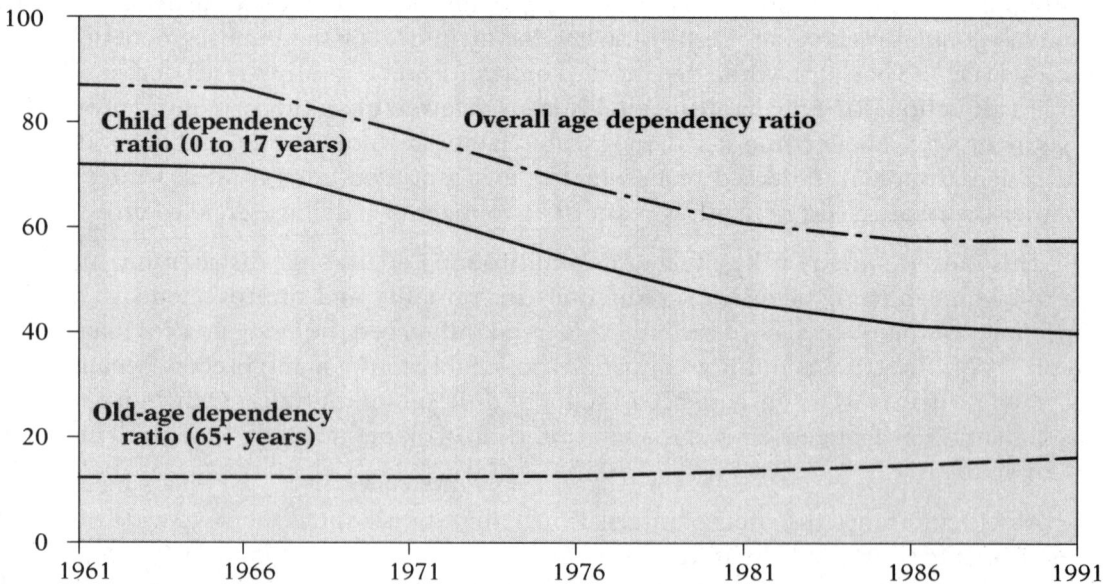

Source: Appendix Table A.2

These ratios, however, only partially reflect actual economic dependency in Canada. For example, many Canadians of working age have no involvement whatsoever in the labour force, while some classified as dependent are involved to a greater or lesser degree. Some Canadians begin their working lives at a very young age, while others retire well before or after age 65. Furthermore, both men and women of working age often depend on public resources (e.g., free medical care), while dependants often provide all sorts of support through family and other networks. Indeed, we are all reliant upon others in a variety of ways. Still, dependency ratios help highlight demographic change, and are often discussed in relation to economic and social policy.

The overall age dependency ratio can be split into two components: the child dependency and the old-age dependency ratios. The decrease in overall dependency is explained entirely by declining child dependency, down from about 73 children per 100 persons of working age in 1961 to only 39 per 100 in 1991. In fact, old-age dependency actually increased, from 14 elderly Canadians per 100 persons of working age in 1961 to about 18 per 100 by 1991.

What are the costs of dependency? The education of children is a major government expense, while a higher proportion moving into their retirement years is associated with more costly government pension plans and higher health care expenses. As sizeable age cohorts make their way toward retirement, the benefits of a low child dependency ratio will soon be offset by the costs associated with sustained increases in old-age dependency.

Regional Differences in Median Age

Although Canada's age structure is now more uniform among regions than in the past, it is worth identifying some of the differences that persist. **Chart 2.5** shows median ages for 1961 and 1991. The median age rose in all regions, but the range of the increase was wide -- from almost 12 years in Newfoundland to only 3.5 years in the Northwest Territories. In explanation of these changes, the effect of fertility is important, overshadowing other factors (such as interprovincial migration). In regions of the country with a modest decline in the birth rate, median age rose modestly (as in Canada's north). In provinces where fertility dropped substantially, the increase in median age was more pronounced (as in Newfoundland). New Brunswick and Quebec also experienced a rather substantial drop in their birth rate, accompanied by a rise in their median age of more than ten years.

In 1991, British Columbia had the highest median age (34.7), followed closely by Quebec (34.2) and Ontario (33.6). Thus, Canada's three most populous provinces are also the "oldest". At the other extreme, the Northwest Territories had by far the youngest median age (24.8), more than 8 years below the national average (33.5). Most of the remaining provinces fell slightly below the national average with much less variation than in 1961.

Chart 2.5
Median Age, Canada, Provinces and Territories, 1961 and 1991

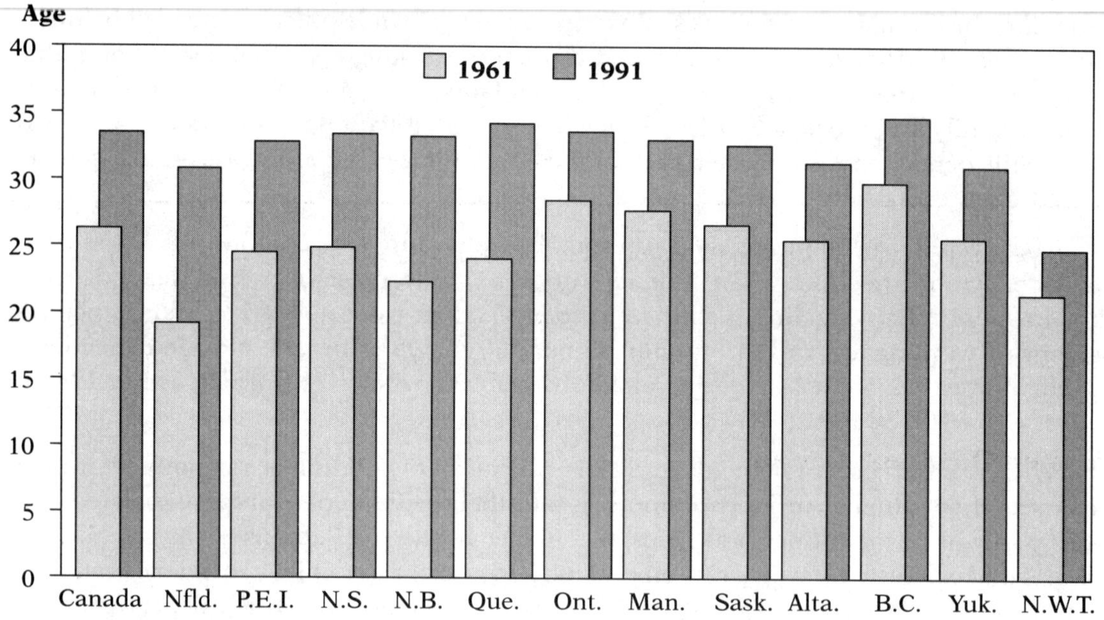

Age
40
35
30
25
20
15
10
5
0
1961
1991
Canada
Nfld.
P.E.I.
N.S.
N.B.
Que.
Ont.
Man.
Sask.
Alta.
B.C.
Yuk.
N.W.T.

Source: Appendix Table A.3

Chapter
3

Sex Composition

Common sense tells us that the number of males and females in Canada is roughly equal. The 1991 Census shows that females actually comprise a slight majority, at 50.7% of the population. However, the relative number of males and females has not remained constant over time, particularly among elderly Canadians.

Women Outnumber Men

The sex ratio is a measure commonly used in discussing Canada's population. This is the ratio of males to females in a population, usually expressed as the number of males per 100 females. Until relatively recently, males outnumbered females (albeit modestly). Canada's sex ratio has steadily fallen from 105 males per 100 females in 1941 to about 97 per 100 in 1991 **(Chart 3.1).** The ratio fell below parity for the first time in the early 1970s. The factors most responsible for this drop include immigration, fertility, and most importantly, mortality.

Historically, males have tended to be more mobile than females. In the decades leading up to the 1960s, the number of males in Canada of foreign birth was consistently higher than the number of females (by 1971, this was no longer true). The effect of fertility is felt through the sex ratio at birth, historically at between 105 and 106 male births to every 100 female births in Canada. A high birth rate contributes to an excess of males while a drop in fertility tilts the balance in favour of females. The impact of mortality is substantial, as the life expectancy for females in Canada is significantly higher than for males (since the early 1960s, life expectancy for females has been 6 to 7 years greater than for males). As more and more Canadians move into their senior years, the sex imbalance at the top of the country's age pyramid increasingly influences the overall sex ratio. If patterns of immigration, mortality and fertility hold, Canada's sex ratio will continue to remain below parity for many years to come.

Chart 3.1
Sex Ratio, Canada, 1941-1991

Males per 100 females

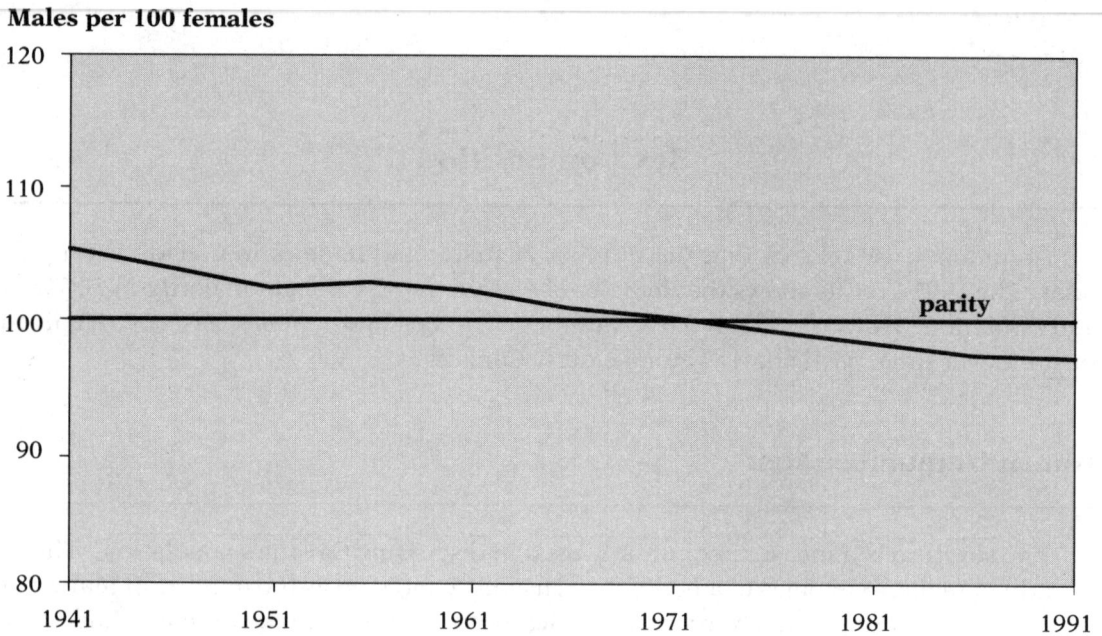

Source: Statistics Canada, *Age, Sex and Marital Status*. 1991 Census of Canada, Catalogue No. 93-310, Table 1.

Imbalance Among Seniors Increasing

While the sex ratio at birth is relatively predictable, the sex ratio of older age groups depends on the level of mortality. As females typically have lower mortality than males, the slight excess of males among the young shifts to a sizeable excess of females among seniors.

This general pattern is seen in **Chart 3.2,** presenting Canada's sex ratio by age in 1991. From infancy to young adulthood, the sex ratio hovers at about 105 males to every 100 females. Up to about age 60, this ratio is around parity; it then declines precipitously as the relative longevity of Canadian women has its effect. By age 70, there are only 80 men to every 100 women. Among those aged 90 and older, women actually outnumber men almost 3 to 1 (36 men to every 100 women).

Chart 3.2
Sex Ratio by Age, Canada, 1991

Males per 100 females

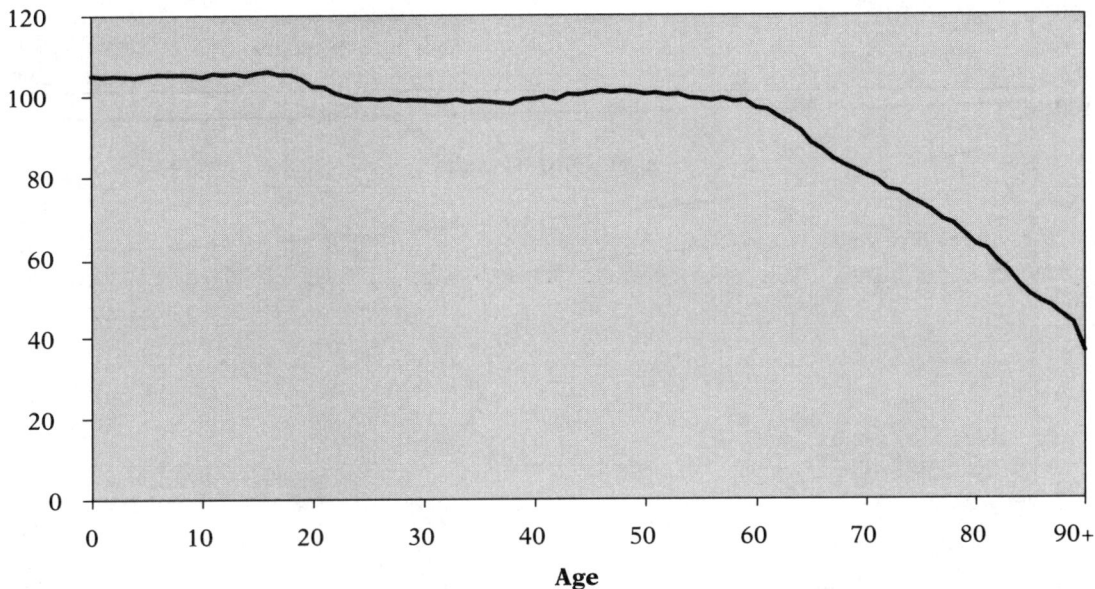

Source: Appendix Table A.1

    In Canada, women at older ages have long outnumbered their male counterparts, but not always to the same degree. **Chart 3.3** demonstrates this fact by focusing on change in the sex ratios of three age groups: children (0 to 14 years), working age Canadians (15 to 64 years) and seniors (65+ years). From 1961 to 1991, the sex ratio of Canadians aged 65 and older dropped significantly, from 94 males per 100 females to 72 per 100, while the two younger age groups had only marginal changes. For children the sex ratio remained virtually unchanged, at about 105, while for working age Canadians it moved from slightly above parity to slightly below.

    Underlying this growing imbalance of the sexes among seniors are two fundamental factors. First, the average age of the population 65 years and older has steadily risen (as a result of lower mortality among older Canadians). Second, the gap between male and female longevity has also widened. This latter trend was particularly pronounced in the 1960s and early 1970s; recently it has stabilized (or even been reversed somewhat). As the aging of the aged has continued, the impact of this mortality gap between men and women has become even more pronounced.

Chart 3.3
Sex Ratio by Selected Age Groups, Canada, 1961-1991

Males per 100 females

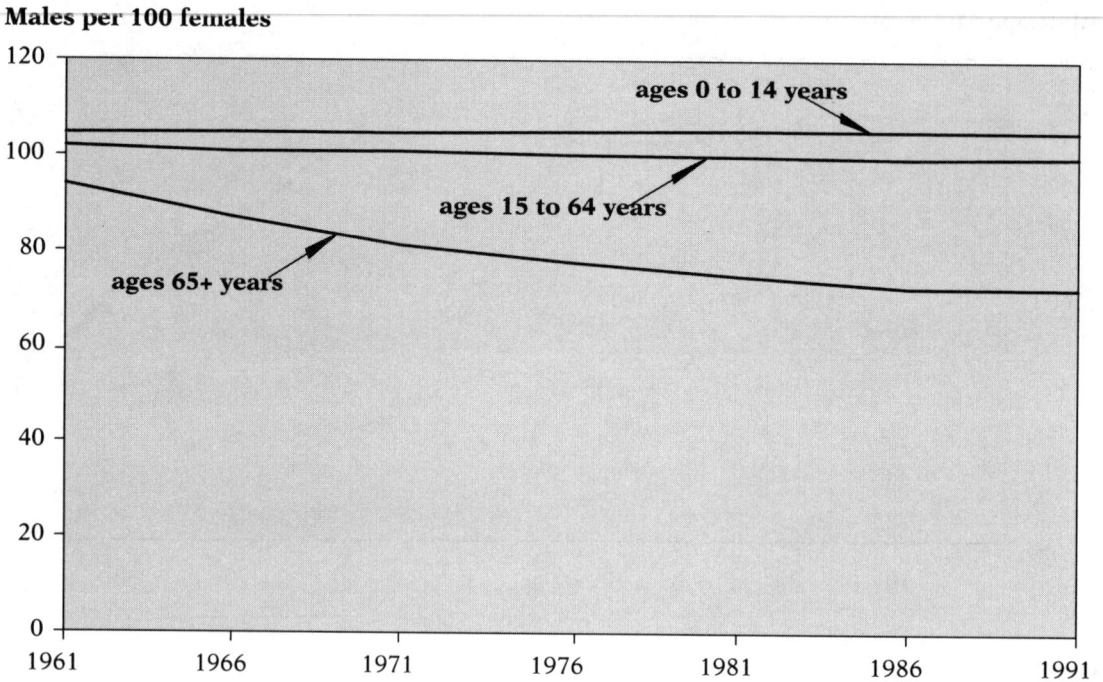

Source: Appendix Table A.1

As **Chart 3.4** shows, the number of elderly women increased substantially faster than the number of elderly men from 1961 to 1991 -- by well over a million for women (from about 717,000 to 1,840,000) compared with about two-thirds of a million for men (from 674,000 to 1,330,000). In other words, in 1961 elderly women outnumbered elderly men by 43,000; by 1991, this had risen to a difference of 509,000. Accommodating this growing discrepancy will place increased pressures on both formal and informal social and economic support systems, since a significant proportion of elderly women are widowed, live alone and are economically less well-off.

This drop in the sex ratio is particularly pronounced among those aged 75 and older **(Chart 3.5).** In this group, the sex ratio declined from 90 males per 100 females in 1961 to only 60 per 100 by 1991. Not only does this substantiate the general impression that there is a preponderance of women among the aged, but even further, that this is more so the case today than in the past. It is unclear whether this longevity gap will get larger, stabilize, or shrink as Canada's population continues to age.

Chart 3.4
Population 65 Years and Over, by Sex, Canada, 1961-1991

Thousands

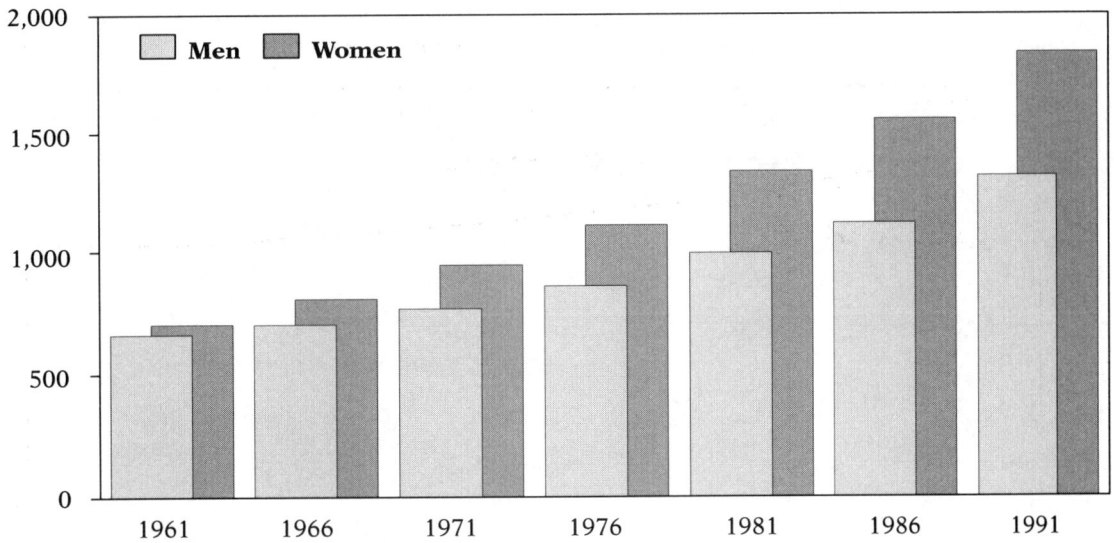

Source: Appendix Table A.1

Chart 3.5
Sex Ratios for Seniors, Canada, 1961-1991

Males per 100 females

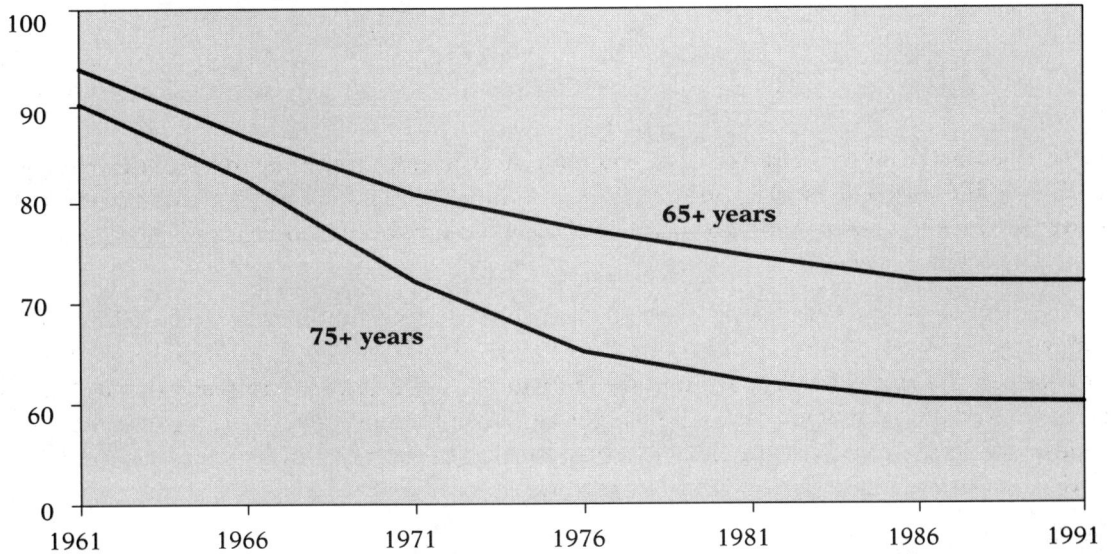

Source: Appendix Table A.1

Chapter

4

Marital Characteristics

The study of marital status is of interest to demographers, largely because of the close link that has historically existed between marriage and childbearing. Although this link is less true today than in the past, still most babies are born to married couples, and most children live with two parents. Although the propensity of Canadians to marry (and stay married) has declined over recent decades, there has been considerable misunderstanding with respect to this trend (at least partially due to the difficulties encountered in measuring the marital characteristics of Canada's population).

One of the reasons for this difficulty is that, in response to societal changes some of the questions about marital status on Canada's census questionnaire have changed over time. For example, a question on common law unions (couples who live together as husband and wife but are not legally married to each other) was not introduced until recently. Still, it is possible to draw a number of meaningful historical comparisons using Census data.

Changing Marriage Patterns

While marriage continues to be a relatively popular institution, for a variety of cultural and economic reasons, Canadians marry less universally, and at older ages. This is reflected in **Chart 4.1,** which shows estimates of the average age at first marriage over past censuses (1941-1991). To facilitate comparisons over time, common-law unions are classified as presently married. Consequently, these estimates not only suggest change in the propensity of Canadians to enter into legal marriage, but more accurately, their propensity to enter in a marital type of arrangement in general.

Chart 4.1
Mean Age at First Marriage, by Sex, Canada, 1941-1991

Age

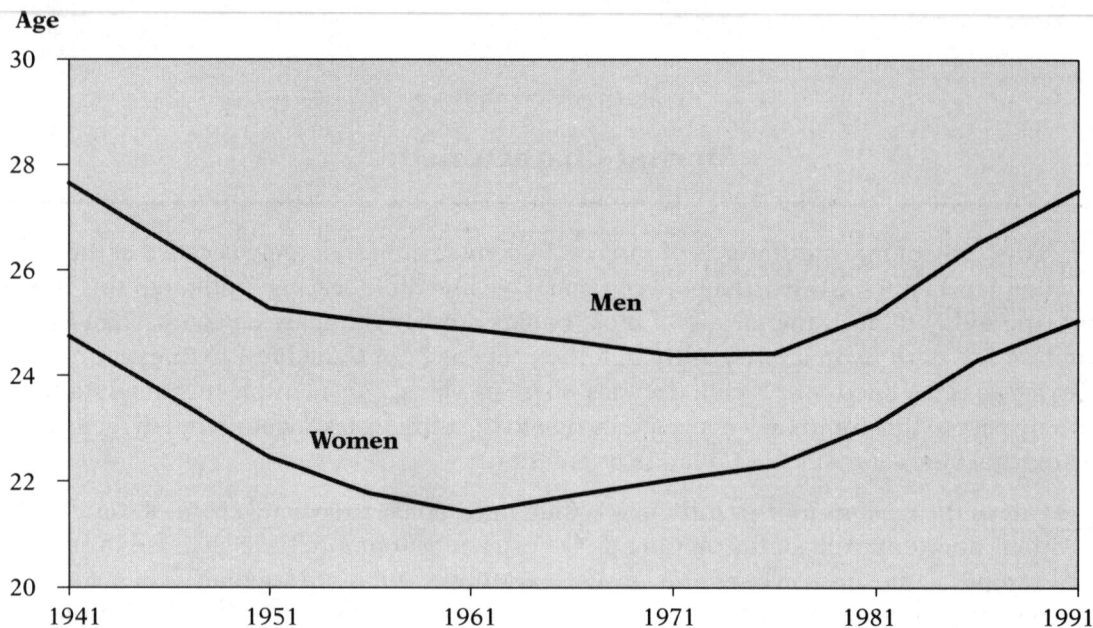

Source: Appendix Table A.4

Average age at first marriage in 1991 was comparable to the average before the post-war baby boom (at just under 28 years of age among males and at about 25 years of age among females). This fact dispels the common belief among Canadians that the further back we move historically, the younger the average age at marriage.

Not surprisingly, as the average age at first marriage gradually increased in the 1970s and 1980s, the relative proportion of single (never-married) young adults also rose **(Chart 4.2)**. The percentage of singles increased significantly over time for three selected age groups of young adults (20 to 24 years, 25 to 29 years and 30 to 34 years). Again, for purposes of this analysis, common-law unions are treated as marriages (in examining marital type arrangements beyond the legal definition).

Consistent with this trend toward delayed marriage, the percentage single among women aged 20 to 24 increased from about 44% in 1971 to 65% by 1991 (while among males, the figures were 68% and 82%, respectively). Among both young men and women, the percentage single almost doubled for the age group 25 to 29 over this same interval. With persons aged 30 to 34, the percentage single recently surpassed 20% among men, while rapidly approaching this mark among women. Considerable growth with respect to the percentage single among the 30 to 34 year age group seems to suggest a growing popularity of alternatives to marriage. Yet in interpretation, it should be noted that these figures can imply either an increased propensity on the part of the young to avoid marriage altogether, and/or an increased propensity on their part to merely delay such an outcome. Overall, this change holds important consequences for family life in Canada, and for the demographic situation in particular.

Chart 4.2
Percentage Never-married (Single)by Selected Age Groups and Sex, Canada, 1971, 1981 and 1991

Percentage

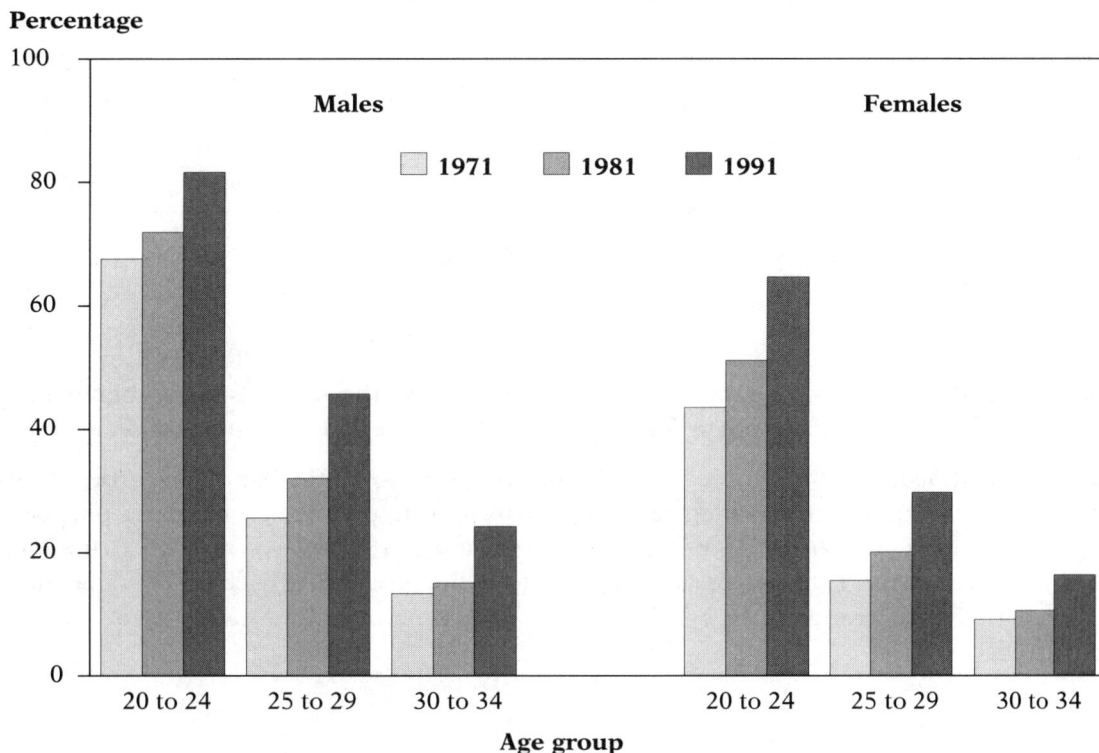

Source: Appendix Table A.5

Recent Trends in Divorce

Divorce leads to another form of "singleness" increasingly prevalent in Canada. The proportion of Canadians divorced and yet to remarry has steadily risen. **Table 4.1** shows the ratio of divorced persons to those currently married (with spouse present) from 1971 to 1991.

Among all persons 15 years and over, this ratio has increased from 19 in 1971 to 69 by 1991. For men, this ratio increased from about 16 to 55 over this same period, while among women, the increase was almost four-fold, from 22 to 83 persons.

Table 4.1
Divorced Persons per 1,000 Married Persons (with Spouse Present) 15 Years and Over, by Sex, Canada, 1971-1991.

Year	All	Males	Females
1971	19	16	22
1976	29	22	35
1981	44	35	52
1986	57	46	69
1991	69	55	83

Source: Appendix Table A.6

Divorce usually is followed by remarriage in Canada, but the likelihood of remarriage has declined. Women have a higher divorce ratio because they are less likely than men to remarry once divorced, and when they do remarry, it is after a longer interval on average.

Chart 4.3 shows the divorce ratio by age from 1971 to 1991. For all age groups, this ratio rose substantially. It has long been highest for the 40 to 49 age group, particularly for women, at about 120 divorcees per 1,000 married women in 1991 compared with 75 per 1,000 married men. The divorce ratio is lower for younger cohorts because they may have been married, on average, for a shorter period of time, and thus fewer divorces have occurred.

Chart 4.3
Divorced Persons per 1,000 Married Persons (with Spouse Present) by Selected Age Groups and Sex, Canada, 1971-1991

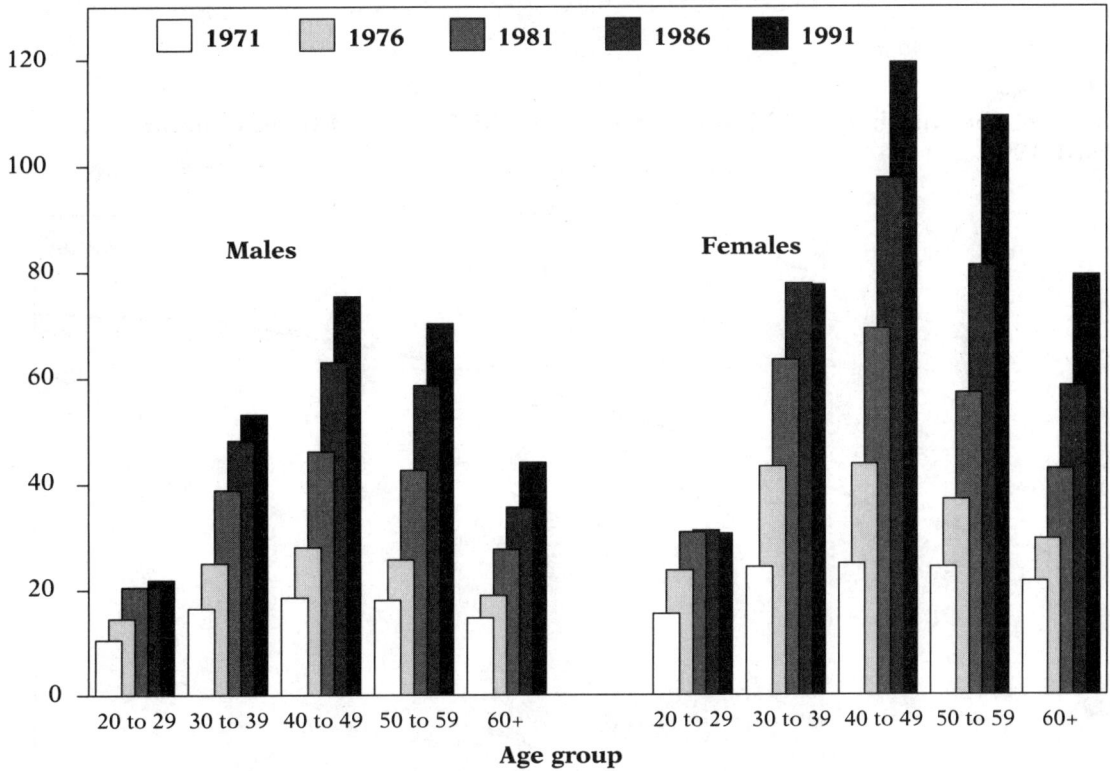

Source: Appendix Table A.6

More Women are Widowed

Since men have higher mortality rates and a shorter life expectancy than women, being left without a spouse is more common among women. As the life expectancy of females has long been 6 to 7 years greater than among males, Canadian women are significantly more likely to experience the death of their spouse. Couples' age differences are also a factor; women, on average, are about two years younger than their partners. A growing number of Canada's elderly women are living as widows for an extended period.

As a direct result of population aging, the number of both widows and widowers has risen, although widowers lag far behind. This phenomenon is demonstrated in **Chart 4.4,** which presents the ratio of widows to widowers over the period 1961-1991. Among Canadians of retirement age, the ratio has risen steadily from under three widows to every one widower in 1961 to five to one by 1991. This occurred because the sex differences in life expectancy increased significantly during the earlier part of this period, and more men remarry after the death of a spouse. Consequently, population aging leads not only to a growing number of Canadians in the retirement ages, but also to a preponderance of elderly women, many of whom are widows.

Chart 4.4
Ratio of the Number of Widows to Widowers, 65 Years and Over, Canada, 1961-1991

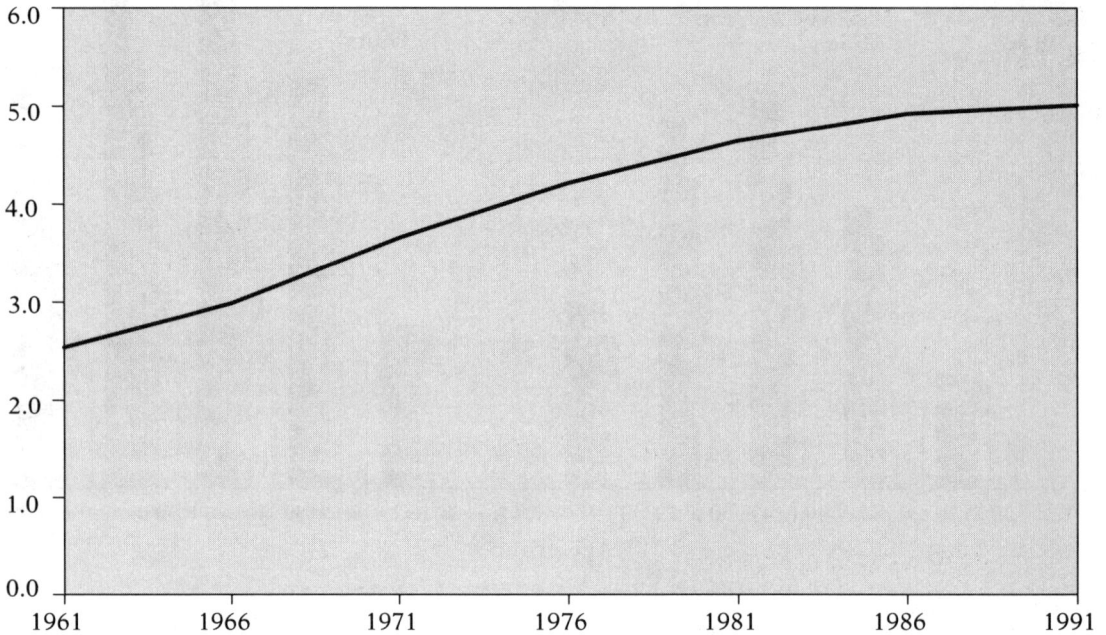

Source: Statistics Canada, *Age, Sex and Marital Status*. 1991 Census of Canada, Catalogue No. 93-310, Table 2.

Common-law Unions Increasingly Popular

Another change with important implications for family life in Canada is the recent increase in the number of common-law unions. Since 1981, the Canadian census has collected information on the prevalence of common-law unions (men and women living together as husband and wife but without legal sanction). As **Chart 4.5** shows, the number of Canadians living common-law grew from about 713,200 in 1981, to 973,900 by 1986, and to 1,451,900 by 1991. The increase was particularly pronounced from 1986 to 1991, climbing 49%.

Although most Canadians living common-law are in younger age groups (with 60% below age 35), common-law unions have become increasingly prevalent among older persons as well **(Chart 4.5).** Growth in the number of Canadians living common law has been slow among persons aged 15 to 24 -- an increase of 11.5% (26,900 persons) from 1981 to 1991. In comparison, by 1991 the number of persons aged 25 to 34 living common-law more than doubled, from about 274,800 in 1981 to 604,200. The total number for the three remaining age groups almost tripled, from about 204,900 in 1981 to 587,300 by 1991.

Chart 4.5
Distribution of Persons in Common-law Unions by Age Group, Canada, 1981, 1986 and 1991

Population ('000)

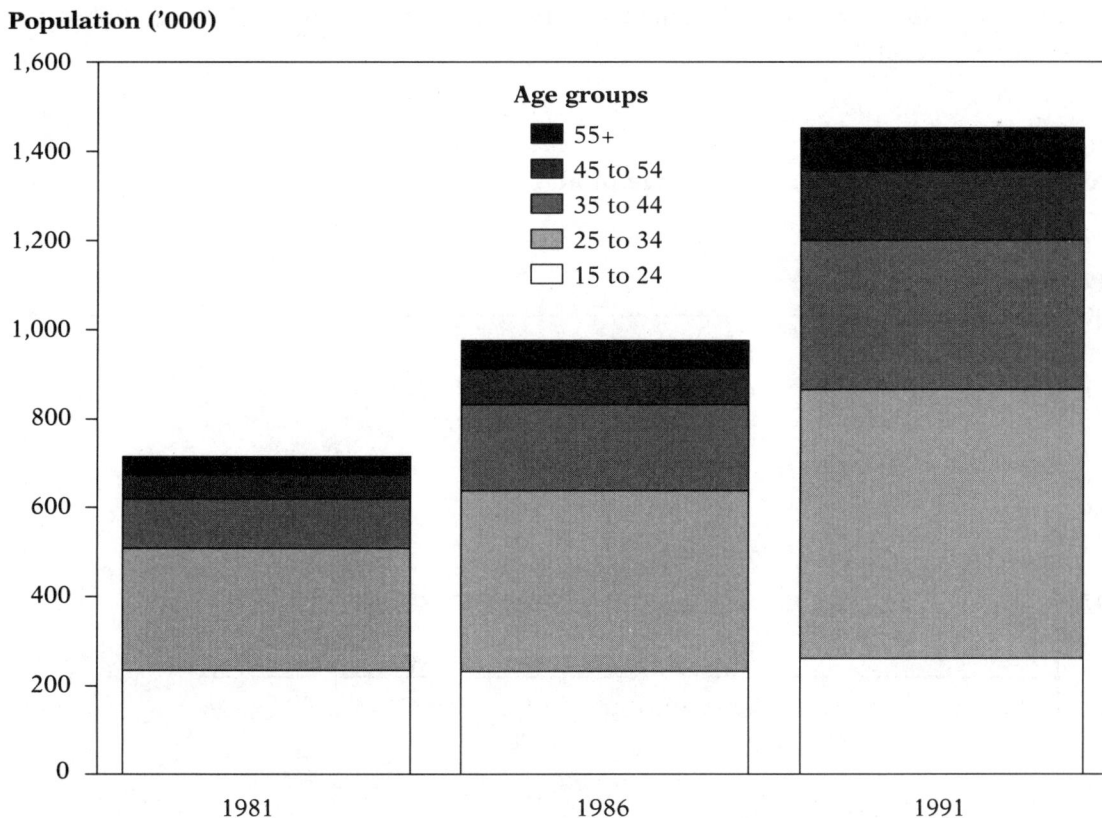

Source: Appendix Table A.7

This distribution, however, is not only influenced by changes in the propensity to live common-law: shifts in the overall age distribution of Canada's population also play a part. The number of Canadians in their middle years has climbed substantially in recent years (as the baby boomers age and the smaller "baby bust" cohorts are now in young adulthood). This shift in age distribution has slowed growth in the number of common-law unions among the particularly young (regardless of changes in the propensity to live common-law), while the opposite can be said for those in their 30s and 40s.

The prevalence of common-law unions varies considerably by region **(Chart 4.6).** Nationally, the percentage of common-law unions among all couples was about 11.3%; Prince Edward Island had the low of 6.9%, while Canada's north was highest (23.4% in the Yukon and 26.5% in the Northwest Territories). Across provinces, Quebec had a significantly higher prevalence than elsewhere (at 19.0%), with British Columbia ranking a distant second (at about 10.9%). Canada's largest province, Ontario, fell well below the national average, at 7.6%.

Chart 4.6
Common-law Unions as a Percentage of all Couples, Canada, Provinces and Territories, 1991

Percentage

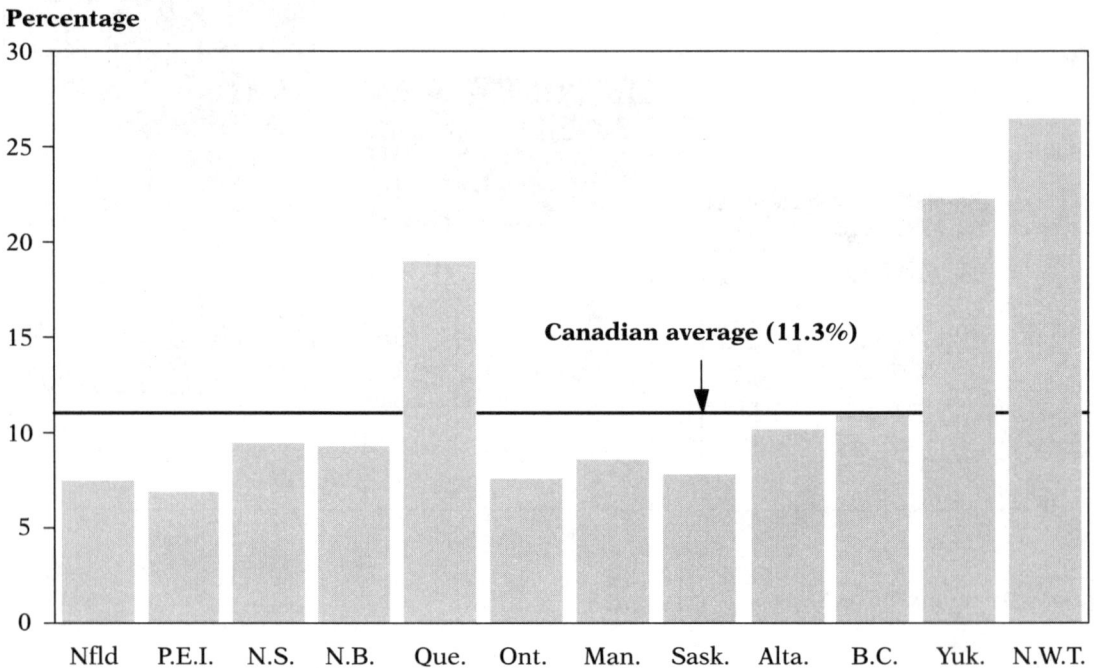

Source: Appendix Table A.8

As Canadians across all age groups choose this lifestyle alternative, of interest is the extent to which this reflects a growing inclination to postpone marriage, or to avoid marriage altogether. **Chart 4.7** shows that 63.6% of all persons living common-law had never been married, 25.9% were legally divorced, and the remainder were either separated (7.1%) or widowed (3.4%).

This distribution varied considerably by age **(Chart 4.8).** Not surprisingly, older age groups are less likely to be never-married and more likely to be divorced or separated. In the 25 to 29 age group, about one in ten were either divorced or separated, compared with about half of those aged 35 to 39. Among middle-aged Canadians living common-law, only a small proportion had never married (for example, only 15.6% among those aged 50 to 54). Among the elderly, over 40% had been widowed before establishing a common-law relationship.

Chart 4.7
Percentage Distribution of Persons 15 Years and Over, Living Common-law, by Legal Marital Status, Canada, 1991

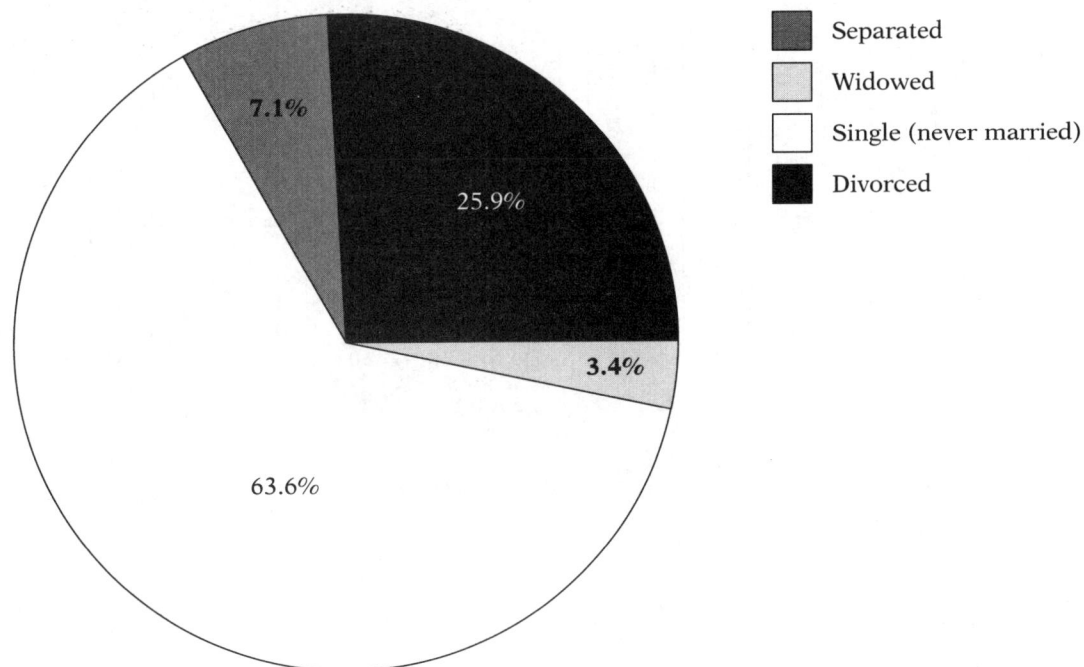

Source: Appendix Table A.9

Chart 4.8
Percentage Distribution of Persons Living in Common-law Unions by Age Group, and Legal Marital Status, Canada, 1991

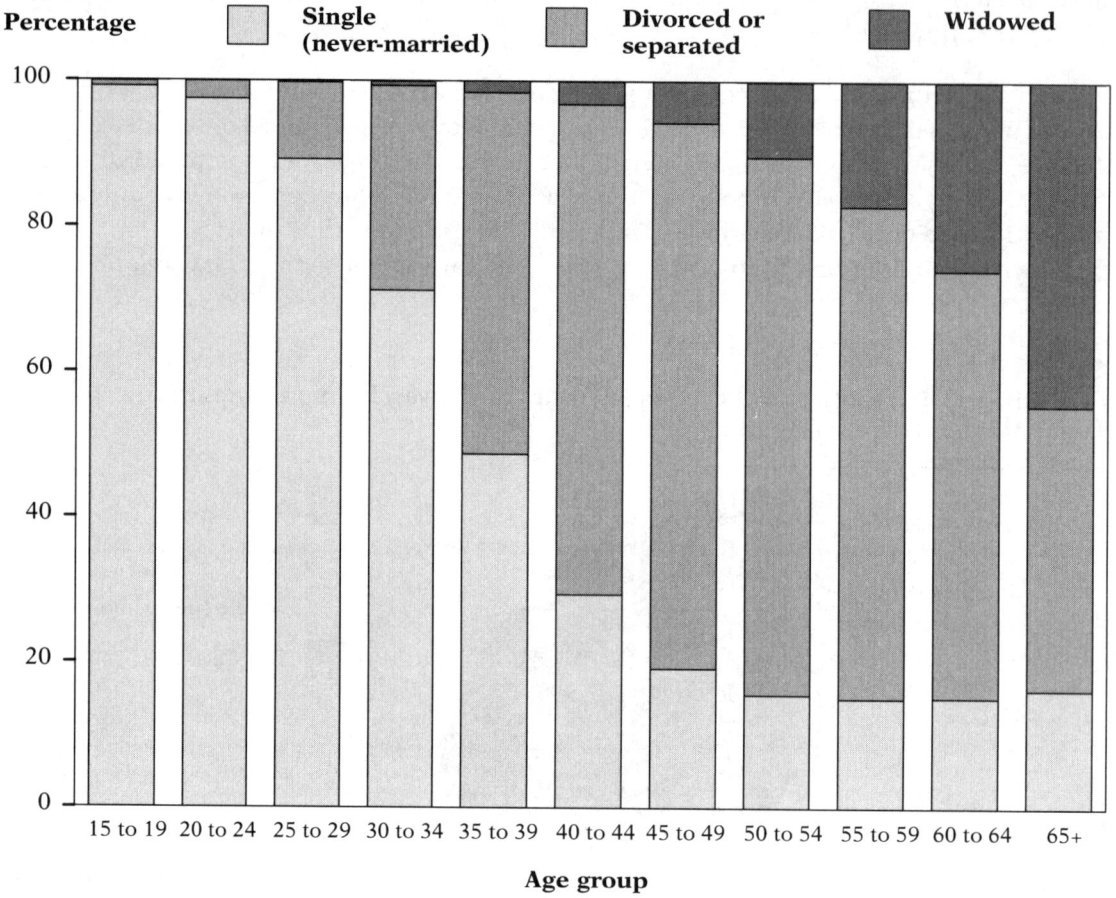

Source: Appendix Table A.9

Conclusion

By analyzing data from Canada's Census, this study has highlighted several fundamental demographic changes influencing the well being of Canadians. These include recent trends in population growth and distribution, and concurrent changes in the marital characteristics, age and sex structure of Canada's population. Will these trends continue, and if so, how can we prepare for the consequences?

While there is some agreement about the future demographic situation in Canada, there is very little about the relationships between demographic change and population policy. Clearly, some demographic trends – such as immigration can be directly influenced by policy changes, although most appear much less responsive to policy interventions. Population analysts disagree over the most appropriate response to population change, and even over which trends are likely to cause problems. Some feel that Canada's population is growing too slowly; others argue that growth is too rapid. For some, population aging is of overwhelming concern.

What will be the implications of demographic change over both the short and long term? As Canada's sizeable baby boom cohorts make their way into retirement, how will Canadians accommodate a dramatic climb in the number of elderly? As women continue to outlive men, what will be the consequences of a growing number of elderly women, many of whom are widowed and living alone? As Canadians choose alternatives to marriage (such as the common-law union), what will be the consequences for all concerned, including children? Hopefully, Census data of the sort highlighted in this report will stimulate further study and debate on these, and other important questions.

Appendix Tables

Table A.1
Population by Single Years of Age and Sex, Canada, 1961-1991

Age and sex		1961	1966	1971	1976	1981	1986	1991
Total	T.	18,238,247	20,014,880	21,568,310	22,992,600	24,343,180	25,309,330	27,296,855
	M.	9,218,893	10,054,344	10,795,370	11,449,525	12,068,290	12,485,650	13,454,580
	F.	9,019,354	9,960,536	10,772,945	11,543,080	12,274,890	12,823,675	13,842,280
0 to 4	T.	2,256,401	2,197,387	1,816,155	1,732,005	1,783,370	1,810,190	1,906,500
	M.	1,154,091	1,128,771	929,600	888,635	914,450	927,785	975,765
	F.	1,102,310	1,068,616	886,545	843,350	868,930	882,420	930,735
Under 1	T.	464,958	400,337	355,870	346,545	363,720	363,625	393,500
	M.	237,879	204,754	182,190	177,695	186,320	186,280	201,600
	F.	227,079	195,583	173,675	168,850	177,400	177,350	191,900
1	T.	456,724	414,532	361,105	347,745	363,405	362,395	394,985
	M.	233,488	212,302	184,630	178,415	186,775	186,375	202,090
	F.	223,236	202,230	176,470	169,320	176,630	176,025	192,895
2	T.	453,560	459,318	354,260	337,295	353,335	361,340	376,335
	M.	232,051	240,634	181,210	172,565	181,070	184,875	192,700
	F.	221,509	218,684	173,050	164,730	172,265	176,465	183,635
3	T.	448,803	462,892	359,070	345,495	349,445	361,755	367,760
	M.	229,246	236,047	183,365	177,565	179,275	185,385	188,185
	F.	219,557	226,845	175,705	167,925	170,175	176,370	179,580
4	T.	432,356	460,308	385,850	354,925	353,465	361,075	373,920
	M.	221,427	235,034	198,205	182,395	181,010	184,870	191,190
	F.	210,929	225,274	187,645	172,525	172,460	176,210	182,725
5 to 9	T.	2,079,522	2,300,857	2,254,000	1,887,810	1,776,860	1,794,980	1,908,035
	M.	1,063,840	1,172,821	1,152,430	966,730	911,940	920,110	978,215
	F.	1,015,682	1,128,036	1,101,575	921,080	864,920	874,880	929,825
5	T.	428,586	469,161	411,370	376,250	355,770	364,275	382,865
	M.	219,276	239,809	208,820	192,705	182,460	186,510	196,135
	F.	209,310	229,352	202,550	183,545	173,310	177,765	186,730
6	T.	423,294	462,672	446,275	376,520	357,610	364,435	383,525
	M.	216,664	236,292	229,765	193,085	183,540	187,025	196,740
	F.	206,630	226,380	216,510	183,435	174,075	177,410	186,785
7	T.	416,490	463,667	459,445	367,055	345,415	356,530	380,980
	M.	213,073	234,121	234,285	188,295	176,780	182,860	195,350
	F.	203,417	229,546	225,160	178,765	168,630	173,675	185,630
8	T.	409,419	459,233	470,950	372,385	354,230	352,225	379,560
	M.	209,376	235,068	241,155	190,420	181,965	180,645	194,600
	F.	200,043	224,165	229,800	181,960	172,265	171,585	184,960

Table A.1
Population by Single Years of Age and Sex, Canada, 1961-1991 (Continued)

Age and sex		1961	1966	1971	1976	1981	1986	1991
9	T.	401,733	446,124	465,960	395,600	363,835	357,515	381,105
	M.	205,451	227,531	238,405	202,225	187,195	183,070	195,390
	F.	196,282	218,593	227,555	193,375	176,640	174,445	185,720
10 to 14	T.	1,855,999	2,093,513	2,310,745	2,276,375	1,920,875	1,786,790	1,878,010
	M.	948,160	1,071,255	1,181,450	1,164,640	984,735	916,755	962,925
	F.	907,839	1,022,258	1,129,285	1,111,730	936,125	870,050	915,090
10	T.	394,116	449,833	471,280	417,165	384,345	356,935	382,755
	M.	201,486	230,204	240,755	213,485	197,045	183,120	195,855
	F.	192,630	219,629	230,525	203,680	187,295	173,815	186,900
11	T.	387,090	429,497	467,975	448,920	383,775	359,475	380,650
	M.	197,774	219,220	239,770	229,750	197,175	184,360	195,430
	F.	189,316	210,277	228,205	219,170	186,595	175,125	185,215
12	T.	376,177	427,544	461,660	464,855	376,820	347,885	373,175
	M.	192,115	221,081	235,845	238,090	193,265	177,945	191,430
	F.	184,062	206,463	225,820	226,765	183,555	169,940	181,750
13	T.	359,444	400,678	458,975	475,280	381,210	357,055	369,230
	M.	183,561	204,037	235,015	242,815	195,105	183,335	189,560
	F.	175,883	196,641	223,955	232,465	186,105	173,725	179,675
14	T.	339,172	385,961	450,855	470,155	394,725	365,440	372,200
	M.	173,224	196,713	230,065	240,500	202,145	187,995	190,650
	F.	165,948	189,248	220,780	229,650	192,575	177,445	181,550
15 to 19	T.	1,432,559	1,837,725	2,114,335	2,345,250	2,314,890	1,924,855	1,868,635
	M.	729,035	928,958	1,074,430	1,195,975	1,182,010	985,260	958,415
	F.	703,524	908,767	1,039,925	1,149,280	1,132,870	939,600	910,235
15	T.	319,756	375,159	445,190	487,120	425,890	391,065	377,240
	M.	163,326	191,641	227,700	249,570	218,400	200,450	193,845
	F.	156,430	183,518	217,490	237,555	207,490	190,610	183,395
16	T.	300,501	367,183	444,235	478,455	462,190	387,425	378,385
	M.	153,594	187,056	226,675	245,080	236,865	199,340	194,705
	F.	146,907	180,127	217,560	233,375	225,320	188,090	183,685
17	T.	283,357	364,994	425,485	466,825	475,955	379,185	365,955
	M.	144,616	184,501	216,275	238,340	244,070	194,885	187,715
	F.	138,741	180,493	209,215	228,485	231,885	184,300	178,245

Table A.1
Population by Single Years of Age and Sex, Canada, 1961-1991 (Continued)

Age and sex		1961	1966	1971	1976	1981	1986	1991
18	T.	269,811	365,648	407,945	459,515	479,805	377,615	370,290
	M.	136,976	183,816	206,685	233,980	244,325	192,685	189,870
	F.	132,835	181,832	201,270	225,535	235,475	184,930	180,425
19	T.	259,134	364,741	391,480	453,335	471,050	389,565	376,765
	M.	130,523	181,944	197,095	229,005	238,350	197,900	192,280
	F.	128,611	182,797	194,390	224,330	232,700	191,670	184,485
20 to 24	T.	1,183,646	1,461,298	1,889,400	2,133,805	2,343,805	2,253,350	1,961,865
	M.	587,139	727,115	941,780	1,065,760	1,174,290	1,131,460	985,215
	F.	596,507	734,183	947,635	1,068,035	1,169,520	1,121,890	976,645
20	T.	248,756	325,196	381,045	446,010	479,415	412,120	393,915
	M.	124,288	161,128	191,255	224,820	241,515	208,440	199,250
	F.	124,468	164,068	189,790	221,190	237,900	203,680	194,665
21	T.	238,734	297,658	371,445	445,505	475,000	446,665	391,995
	M.	118,148	150,068	186,165	222,925	239,020	225,005	198,180
	F.	120,586	147,590	185,285	222,575	235,980	221,665	193,815
22	T.	232,371	288,451	370,315	425,230	464,885	460,275	386,115
	M.	114,438	141,838	184,870	211,660	232,295	231,350	193,780
	F.	117,933	146,613	185,450	213,565	232,590	228,925	192,330
23	T.	230,910	284,883	376,205	413,295	464,060	468,805	388,345
	M.	114,130	142,235	188,365	205,130	232,035	234,525	194,055
	F.	116,780	142,648	187,835	208,160	232,025	234,275	194,290
24	T.	232,875	265,110	390,390	403,765	460,445	465,485	401,495
	M.	116,135	131,846	191,125	201,225	229,425	232,140	199,950
	F.	116,740	133,264	199,275	202,545	231,025	233,345	201,545
25 to 29	T.	1,209,297	1,241,794	1,584,120	1,993,060	2,177,605	2,341,505	2,375,540
	M.	613,897	619,462	800,710	1,000,525	1,084,415	1,164,985	1,182,570
	F.	595,400	622,332	783,410	992,540	1,093,200	1,176,520	1,192,955
25	T.	235,424	268,097	329,810	400,095	446,885	475,225	429,170
	M.	118,331	133,954	166,065	200,565	223,335	237,335	213,865
	F.	117,093	134,143	163,745	199,530	223,550	237,890	215,305
26	T.	238,929	247,499	323,085	395,030	450,910	471,560	468,135
	M.	121,053	123,046	159,635	198,595	224,140	235,085	233,025
	F.	117,876	124,453	163,450	196,430	226,775	236,475	235,110
27	T.	242,443	251,192	323,325	394,000	438,905	465,345	485,350
	M.	123,498	124,025	167,030	197,250	218,100	231,175	241,870
	F.	118,945	127,167	156,295	196,750	220,805	234,170	243,475

Table A.1
Population by Single Years of Age and Sex, Canada, 1961-1991 (Continued)

Age and sex		1961	1966	1971	1976	1981	1986	1991
28	T.	245,155	245,203	312,090	398,180	425,285	465,795	497,285
	M.	125,040	122,967	155,760	200,030	211,305	231,400	247,305
	F.	120,115	122,236	156,330	198,155	213,980	234,395	249,975
29	T.	247,346	229,803	295,810	405,755	415,620	463,580	495,600
	M.	125,975	115,470	152,220	204,085	207,535	229,990	246,505
	F.	121,371	114,333	143,590	201,675	208,090	233,590	249,090
30 to 34	T.	1,271,810	1,241,697	1,305,420	1,627,485	2,038,585	2,185,645	2,491,045
	M.	644,407	630,498	660,880	822,690	1,021,480	1,083,765	1,237,685
	F.	627,403	611,199	644,555	804,795	1,017,100	1,101,880	1,253,365
30	T.	249,967	268,848	276,690	347,360	412,690	450,730	507,065
	M.	127,212	135,841	138,955	175,345	206,325	223,890	252,110
	F.	122,755	133,007	137,740	172,015	206,365	226,840	254,955
31	T.	252,664	224,580	266,625	333,580	405,360	452,935	502,720
	M.	128,550	112,794	136,010	168,820	203,220	224,545	249,660
	F.	124,114	111,786	130,615	164,760	202,140	228,390	253,060
32	T.	254,950	245,394	260,520	330,205	402,985	440,935	496,040
	M.	129,447	123,939	131,350	166,705	201,370	218,075	246,330
	F.	125,503	121,455	129,175	163,500	201,610	222,865	249,715
33	T.	256,629	255,248	254,515	320,830	406,530	427,330	495,925
	M.	129,727	131,059	129,905	162,205	204,050	211,575	246,810
	F.	126,902	124,189	124,610	158,630	202,480	215,750	249,115
34	T.	257,600	247,627	247,070	295,510	411,020	413,715	489,295
	M.	129,471	126,865	124,660	149,615	206,515	205,680	242,775
	F.	128,129	120,762	122,415	145,890	204,505	208,035	246,520
35 to 39	T.	1,270,924	1,286,144	1,263,870	1,328,780	1,630,250	2,026,180	2,284,475
	M.	631,072	649,769	645,045	671,340	822,295	1,011,050	1,133,670
	F.	639,852	636,375	618,815	657,450	807,950	1,015,120	1,150,805
35	T.	258,290	266,717	252,590	284,450	352,200	410,015	473,045
	M.	129,087	134,715	128,645	143,850	177,460	204,325	234,955
	F.	129,203	132,002	123,945	140,605	174,735	205,685	238,085
36	T.	258,985	255,273	248,125	271,000	332,440	403,105	475,550
	M.	128,653	128,809	125,930	136,645	167,865	201,180	235,985
	F.	130,332	126,464	122,195	134,360	164,570	201,925	239,565
37	T.	257,227	259,250	247,905	265,545	327,665	401,205	460,905
	M.	127,303	131,948	126,845	134,295	165,110	199,730	228,320
	F.	129,924	127,302	121,060	131,250	162,560	201,470	232,590

Table A.1
Population by Single Years of Age and Sex, Canada, 1961-1991 (Continued)

Age and sex		1961	1966	1971	1976	1981	1986	1991
38	T.	251,973	258,714	257,865	256,160	320,430	403,295	443,415
	M.	124,710	130,778	131,280	129,550	161,600	201,510	219,505
	F.	127,263	127,936	126,580	126,610	158,830	201,785	223,910
39	T.	244,449	246,190	257,385	251,625	297,515	408,560	431,560
	M.	121,319	123,519	132,345	127,000	150,260	204,305	214,905
	F.	123,130	122,671	125,035	124,625	147,255	204,255	216,655
40 to 44	T.	1,118,961	1,257,028	1,262,530	1,268,220	1,337,900	1,614,720	2,086,905
	M.	559,996	624,709	640,770	643,575	674,675	810,935	1,042,185
	F.	558,965	632,319	621,760	624,640	663,240	803,785	1,044,710
40	T.	236,804	283,354	253,860	253,745	288,395	349,670	426,250
	M.	117,829	140,402	129,870	128,505	145,235	175,320	212,320
	F.	118,975	142,952	123,995	125,235	143,165	174,350	213,930
41	T.	228,409	229,827	256,195	249,655	273,270	329,645	418,155
	M.	113,987	114,297	130,875	126,250	137,595	165,890	208,875
	F.	114,422	115,530	125,320	123,405	135,680	163,755	209,275
42	T.	221,509	268,868	249,925	250,250	267,580	324,940	412,990
	M.	110,896	134,339	126,740	127,100	135,010	163,275	205,590
	F.	110,613	134,529	123,185	123,145	132,565	161,665	207,400
43	T.	217,364	244,175	253,825	259,765	257,605	316,945	413,130
	M.	109,130	121,515	128,420	131,645	130,230	158,945	206,955
	F.	108,234	122,660	125,400	128,120	127,380	158,000	206,175
44	T.	214,875	230,804	248,725	254,805	251,050	293,520	416,380
	M.	108,154	114,156	124,865	130,075	126,605	147,505	208,445
	F.	106,721	116,648	123,860	124,735	124,450	146,015	207,930
45 to 49	T.	1,015,316	1,089,915	1,239,040	1,252,845	1,255,350	1,315,885	1,640,790
	M.	515,516	542,752	613,410	630,470	634,705	659,970	824,200
	F.	499,800	547,163	625,625	622,375	620,645	655,910	816,585
45	T.	211,736	251,651	250,875	255,085	253,970	283,595	356,785
	M.	106,893	125,172	125,080	129,510	128,090	142,100	178,975
	F.	104,843	126,479	125,795	125,570	125,875	141,495	177,805
46	T.	208,496	224,931	249,275	255,980	249,110	269,100	336,785
	M.	105,598	111,855	123,540	129,620	125,540	134,760	169,370
	F.	102,898	113,076	125,735	126,360	123,570	134,340	167,415
47	T.	204,346	210,312	248,360	246,770	243,815	262,550	329,050
	M.	103,805	103,167	122,815	124,095	123,360	131,980	165,205
	F.	100,541	107,145	125,545	122,680	120,455	130,565	163,845

Table A.1
Population by Single Years of Age and Sex, Canada, 1961-1991 (Continued)

Age and sex		1961	1966	1971	1976	1981	1986	1991
48	T.	198,691	204,077	242,820	249,170	253,950	252,930	320,190
	M.	101,193	101,168	119,520	124,825	128,510	127,035	160,995
	F.	97,498	102,909	123,295	124,345	125,440	125,895	159,195
49	T.	192,047	198,944	247,710	245,840	254,505	247,710	297,980
	M.	98,027	101,390	122,455	122,420	129,205	124,095	149,655
	F.	94,020	97,554	125,255	123,420	125,305	123,615	148,325
50 to 54	T.	863,188	988,264	1,052,550	1,220,185	1,243,475	1,229,330	1,325,460
	M.	442,909	498,283	518,900	595,710	621,660	616,195	663,285
	F.	420,279	489,981	533,635	624,465	621,810	613,135	662,175
50	T.	185,593	225,288	232,020	248,395	255,680	249,935	288,315
	M.	94,937	112,012	114,300	122,375	129,005	125,170	144,420
	F.	90,656	113,276	117,715	126,020	126,675	124,770	143,900
51	T.	179,176	185,742	224,670	245,550	254,980	243,565	271,135
	M.	91,837	93,753	111,360	120,370	128,205	121,760	135,975
	F.	87,339	91,989	113,305	125,175	126,775	121,805	135,160
52	T.	172,660	207,308	203,295	242,140	244,625	239,285	264,945
	M.	88,643	104,747	99,645	118,075	122,540	120,080	132,565
	F.	84,017	102,561	103,650	124,060	122,085	119,200	132,375
53	T.	166,127	191,755	197,280	241,420	246,800	248,485	254,350
	M.	85,388	97,533	97,145	117,005	122,665	124,655	127,375
	F.	80,739	94,222	100,135	124,415	124,135	123,830	126,975
54	T.	159,632	178,171	195,285	242,680	241,390	248,060	246,715
	M.	82,104	90,238	96,450	117,885	119,245	124,530	122,950
	F.	77,528	87,933	98,830	124,795	122,140	123,530	123,765
55 to 59	T.	705,835	816,300	954,725	1,019,030	1,179,915	1,203,195	1,222,920
	M.	362,145	413,389	472,415	492,260	568,395	593,605	608,080
	F.	343,690	402,911	482,320	526,780	611,535	609,595	614,835
55	T.	153,130	182,436	194,540	227,605	243,090	248,510	249,110
	M.	78,788	92,458	96,200	110,160	118,515	123,870	124,030
	F.	74,342	89,978	98,345	117,445	124,575	124,640	125,080
56	T.	146,621	166,273	201,630	220,020	239,760	246,490	243,475
	M.	75,457	84,702	99,610	106,800	116,210	122,535	120,985
	F.	71,164	81,571	102,025	113,220	123,555	123,960	122,490
57	T.	140,568	162,727	195,405	195,185	235,950	236,665	238,330
	M.	72,252	82,098	97,020	94,000	113,485	116,840	118,750
	F.	68,316	80,629	98,390	101,185	122,465	119,830	119,575

Table A.1
Population by Single Years of Age and Sex, Canada, 1961-1991 (Continued)

Age and sex		1961	1966	1971	1976	1981	1986	1991
58	T.	135,194	160,548	185,010	188,420	229,715	238,150	245,185
	M.	69,245	81,025	91,450	90,865	109,905	116,785	121,680
	F.	65,949	79,523	93,560	97,555	119,815	121,360	123,505
59	T.	130,322	144,316	178,140	187,800	231,400	233,380	246,820
	M.	66,403	73,106	88,135	90,435	110,280	113,575	122,635
	F.	63,919	71,210	90,000	97,375	121,125	119,805	124,185
60 to 64	T.	583,635	663,410	777,010	905,405	979,325	1,125,130	1,176,705
	M.	292,569	330,006	381,690	435,790	462,390	530,455	571,935
	F.	291,066	333,404	395,320	469,615	516,930	594,665	604,765
60	T.	125,536	153,552	169,070	186,620	221,955	233,655	245,945
	M.	63,604	75,780	83,380	90,160	105,345	111,855	121,050
	F.	61,932	77,772	85,695	96,460	116,610	121,805	124,900
61	T.	120,895	123,856	160,305	190,590	213,370	229,140	241,340
	M.	60,858	62,301	79,885	91,885	101,385	108,955	118,530
	F.	60,037	61,555	80,420	98,705	111,985	120,185	122,805
62	T.	116,493	139,535	155,055	183,635	185,670	224,580	231,530
	M.	58,297	68,327	76,210	88,480	87,310	105,705	112,605
	F.	58,196	71,208	78,845	95,155	98,360	118,875	118,925
63	T.	112,335	129,565	149,890	174,325	179,375	218,175	231,715
	M.	55,976	64,478	73,300	83,855	84,605	101,920	111,775
	F.	56,359	65,087	76,590	90,470	94,770	116,245	119,940
64	T.	108,376	116,902	142,690	170,235	178,955	219,580	226,175
	M.	53,834	59,120	68,915	81,410	83,745	102,020	107,975
	F.	54,542	57,782	73,770	88,825	95,205	117,555	118,195
65 to 69	T.	487,102	531,709	619,960	720,810	844,330	911,765	1,073,170
	M.	239,685	254,938	296,050	338,520	390,580	414,545	492,490
	F.	247,417	276,771	323,905	382,300	453,745	497,220	580,655
65	T.	104,503	123,717	136,890	162,150	178,515	210,145	226,170
	M.	51,731	60,288	65,485	76,765	83,330	96,625	106,035
	F.	52,772	63,429	71,405	85,390	95,185	113,510	120,130
66	T.	100,632	108,462	131,345	150,730	180,560	200,525	220,305
	M.	49,643	53,129	62,670	71,990	83,780	91,925	102,280
	F.	50,989	55,333	68,675	78,740	96,780	108,600	118,020
67	T.	97,068	105,389	124,825	143,270	172,370	172,750	214,200
	M.	47,734	50,595	59,870	67,075	79,940	78,160	98,050
	F.	49,334	54,794	64,950	76,195	92,425	94,595	116,150

Table A.1
Population by Single Years of Age and Sex, Canada, 1961-1991 (Continued)

Age and sex		1961	1966	1971	1976	1981	1986	1991
68	T.	93,924	98,985	117,735	136,895	162,335	165,705	206,865
	M.	46,061	46,546	56,165	63,865	74,680	75,090	93,740
	F.	47,863	52,439	61,575	73,035	87,660	90,620	113,120
69	T.	90,975	95,156	109,165	127,765	150,550	162,640	205,630
	M.	44,516	44,380	51,860	58,825	68,850	72,745	92,385
	F.	46,459	50,776	57,300	68,940	81,695	89,895	113,235
70 to 74	T.	402,175	427,207	457,385	533,725	633,420	738,325	821,895
	M.	196,076	198,808	205,570	241,360	281,225	324,335	358,955
	F.	206,099	228,399	251,805	292,370	352,185	413,990	462,945
70	T.	87,974	102,932	103,845	120,720	143,710	159,700	194,480
	M.	42,959	46,562	48,035	55,190	64,805	71,385	86,555
	F.	45,015	56,370	55,810	65,530	78,900	88,310	107,925
71	T.	85,058	80,721	98,030	114,180	135,750	159,865	182,980
	M.	41,452	37,864	44,885	51,860	61,480	70,920	80,785
	F.	43,606	42,857	53,140	62,325	74,275	88,945	102,195
72	T.	81,407	92,585	90,885	107,400	126,185	150,525	155,340
	M.	39,634	43,867	40,715	48,680	55,810	66,030	67,445
	F.	41,773	48,718	50,170	58,720	70,375	84,500	87,900
73	T.	76,632	79,031	84,315	100,120	118,605	140,210	147,245
	M.	37,333	36,850	37,075	44,995	51,985	61,035	63,690
	F.	39,299	42,181	47,235	55,125	66,615	79,170	83,555
74	T.	71,104	71,938	80,310	91,305	109,170	128,025	141,850
	M.	34,698	33,665	34,860	40,635	47,145	54,965	60,480
	F.	36,406	38,273	45,450	50,670	62,020	73,065	81,370
75 to 79	T.	274,237	300,365	325,505	362,700	432,665	510,355	614,775
	M.	134,186	138,967	140,005	150,430	180,485	209,905	252,535
	F.	140,051	161,398	185,515	212,275	252,175	300,450	362,245
75	T.	65,695	72,618	76,050	87,845	101,950	120,340	137,360
	M.	32,133	33,170	32,905	37,670	43,195	50,755	57,975
	F.	33,562	39,448	43,150	50,175	58,750	69,580	79,385
76	T.	60,284	64,592	69,580	79,835	94,390	111,050	135,660
	M.	29,585	30,008	29,890	33,810	39,715	46,700	56,515
	F.	30,699	34,584	39,695	46,025	54,675	64,350	79,150
77	T.	54,825	60,597	64,995	71,345	87,120	101,415	125,235
	M.	26,935	28,281	27,940	29,420	36,225	41,600	51,235
	F.	27,890	32,316	37,055	41,930	50,900	59,815	74,005

Table A.1
Population by Single Years of Age and Sex, Canada, 1961-1991 (Continued)

Age and sex		1961	1966	1971	1976	1981	1986	1991
78	T.	49,392	55,558	60,110	63,795	78,915	93,330	113,875
	M.	24,169	25,825	25,795	25,755	32,625	37,625	46,145
	F.	25,223	29,733	34,315	38,035	46,285	55,705	67,730
79	T.	44,041	47,000	54,770	59,880	70,290	84,220	102,645
	M.	21,364	21,683	23,475	23,775	28,725	33,225	40,665
	F.	22,677	25,317	31,300	36,110	41,565	51,000	61,975
80 to 84	T.	146,817	177,319	204,180	220,560	256,795	309,370	376,790
	M.	69,046	80,664	85,680	85,245	94,935	115,355	140,135
	F.	77,771	96,655	118,490	135,310	161,855	194,015	236,665
80	T.	38,760	47,539	49,035	54,945	64,930	76,805	93,995
	M.	18,612	21,429	20,835	21,555	25,170	29,450	36,355
	F.	20,148	26,110	28,195	33,385	39,760	47,355	57,650
81	T.	33,558	36,643	44,825	48,495	57,355	69,135	83,960
	M.	15,894	17,126	18,940	18,955	21,820	26,070	32,125
	F.	17,664	19,517	25,885	29,540	35,530	43,070	51,840
82	T.	28,796	35,642	42,140	43,440	50,085	61,910	74,365
	M.	13,450	16,202	17,560	16,820	18,370	23,010	27,550
	F.	15,346	19,440	24,580	26,625	31,715	38,895	46,810
83	T.	24,661	31,157	36,830	39,435	44,500	54,530	66,725
	M.	11,408	14,149	15,390	14,935	15,780	20,015	24,080
	F.	13,253	17,008	21,435	24,495	28,720	34,515	42,645
84	T.	21,042	26,338	31,350	34,245	39,925	46,990	57,745
	M.	9,682	11,758	12,955	12,980	13,795	16,810	20,025
	F.	11,360	14,580	18,395	21,265	26,130	30,180	37,720
85 to 89	T.	60,784	76,790	100,005	112,380	130,940	152,135	189,490
	M.	27,178	33,073	40,625	41,475	44,030	48,520	61,255
	F.	33,606	43,717	59,385	70,900	86,910	103,610	128,235
85	T.	17,648	22,609	28,010	30,030	35,370	41,740	50,360
	M.	8,052	9,729	11,535	11,295	12,195	14,065	16,920
	F.	9,596	12,880	16,475	18,735	23,180	27,675	33,435
86	T.	14,543	19,020	23,695	26,255	30,515	35,410	44,070
	M.	6,563	8,339	9,810	9,760	10,370	11,695	14,500
	F.	7,980	10,681	13,885	16,495	20,140	23,710	29,570
87	T.	11,793	14,459	19,570	22,910	25,460	29,275	37,575
	M.	5,254	6,221	7,925	8,400	8,495	9,205	12,125
	F.	6,539	8,238	11,645	14,505	16,965	20,070	25,450

Table A.1
Population by Single Years of Age and Sex, Canada, 1961-1991 (Concluded)

Age and sex		1961	1966	1971	1976	1981	1986	1991
88	T.	9,408	11,499	15,940	18,540	21,625	24,755	31,520
	M.	4,127	4,932	6,335	6,680	7,085	7,535	9,855
	F.	5,281	6,567	9,610	11,860	14,535	17,220	21,670
89	T.	7,392	9,203	12,790	14,645	17,970	20,955	25,965
	M.	3,182	3,852	5,020	5,340	5,885	6,020	7,855
	F.	4,210	5,351	7,770	9,305	12,090	14,935	18,110
90+	T.	20,039	26,158	37,380	52,170	62,840	75,630	93,845
	M.	7,946	10,106	13,940	18,360	19,615	20,675	25,055
	F.	12,093	16,052	23,445	33,795	43,230	54,945	68,795

Sources: Statistics Canada, 1961 Census of Canada, Vol. 1, Part 2, Table 26.

Statistics Canada, 1966 Census of Canada, Vol. 1, Table 25.

Statistics Canada, *Single Years of Age.* 1971 Census of Canada, Catalogue No. 92-716, Table 14.

Statistics Canada, *Single Years of Age.* 1976 Census of Canada, Catalogue No. 92-832, Table 1.

Statistics Canada, *Age, Sex and Marital Status.* 1981 Census of Canada, Catalogue No. 92-901, Table 2.

Statistics Canada, *Age, Sex and Marital Status.* 1986 Census of Canada, Catalogue No. 93-101, Table 4.

Statistics Canada, *Age, Sex and Marital Status.* 1991 Census of Canada, Catalogue No. 93-310, Table 4.

Table A.2
Population by Selected Age Groups and Total Dependency Ratios, Canada
1961-1991

	1961	1966	1971	1976	1981	1986	1991
Population							
All ages	**18,238,247**	**20,014,880**	**21,568,310**	**22,992,600**	**24,343,180**	**25,309,330**	**27,296,855**
0 to 17 years	7,095,536	7,699,093	7,695,810	7,328,590	6,845,140	6,549,635	6,814,140
18 to 64 years	9,751,557	10,776,239	12,128,090	13,661,665	15,137,065	16,062,120	17,312,740
65+	1,391,154	1,539,548	1,744,415	2,002,345	2,360,990	2,697,580	3,169,940
Total dependency ratios							
Age dependency[1]	87.0	85.7	77.8	68.3	60.8	57.6	57.7
Child dependency[2]	72.8	71.4	63.5	53.6	45.2	40.8	39.4
Old-age dependency[3]	14.3	14.3	14.4	14.7	15.6	16.8	18.3

[1] (0 to 17 years age group + 65 years and over age group)/(18 to 64 years age group) x 100

[2] (0 to 17 years age group)/(18 to 64 years age group) x 100

[3] (65 years and over age group)/(18 to 64 years age group) x 100

Source: Calculated from Appendix Table A.1

Table A.3
Median Age, Canada, Provinces and Territories, 1961-1991

	1961	1966	1971	1976	1981	1986	1991
Canada	**26.3**	**25.4**	**26.3**	**27.8**	**29.6**	**31.6**	**33.5**
Newfoundland	19.1	19.3	20.7	22.6	25.2	27.9	30.8
Prince Edward Island	24.5	24.0	24.8	26.6	28.8	30.6	32.8
Nova Scotia	24.9	24.6	25.4	27.1	29.3	31.2	33.4
New Brunswick	22.3	22.2	23.9	25.7	28.1	30.5	33.2
Quebec	24.0	23.9	25.6	27.7	29.7	32.0	34.2
Ontario	28.4	27.2	27.2	28.6	30.6	32.3	33.6
Manitoba	27.7	26.7	26.8	28.0	29.9	31.4	33.0
Saskatchewan	26.6	25.5	26.7	27.6	28.7	30.1	32.6
Alberta	25.5	24.5	24.9	26.1	26.9	29.2	31.3
British Columbia	29.8	28.2	27.9	29.1	30.9	33.1	34.7
Yukon	25.6	23.6	24.1	24.9	26.6	28.9	31.0
Northwest Territories	21.4	19.5	19.1	20.6	22.0	23.7	24.8

Sources: Calculated from: Statistics Canada, 1961 Census of Canada, Vol.1, Part 2, Table 26.

Calculated from: Statistics Canada, 1966 Census of Canada, Vol.1, Table 25.

Calculated from: Statistics Canada, *Single Years of Age.* 1971 Census of Canada, Catalogue No. 92-716, Table 14.

Statistics Canada, *Single Years of Age.* 1976 Census of Canada, Catalogue No. 92-832, Table 1.

Statistics Canada, *Age, Sex and Marital Status.* 1981 Census of Canada, Catalogue No. 92-901, Table 2.

Statistics Canada, *Age, Sex and Marital Status.* 1986 Census of Canada, Catalogue No. 93-101, Table 4.

Statistics Canada, *Age, Sex and Marital Status.* 1991 Census of Canada, Catalogue No. 93-310, Table 4.

Table A.4
Mean Age At First Marriage[1] by Sex, Canada, 1941–1991

Census year	Male	Female
1941	27.7	24.8
1946	N.A	N.A
1951	25.3	22.5
1956	25.0	21.8
1961	24.8	21.4
1966	24.7	21.8
1971	24.4	22.0
1976	24.4	22.3
1981	25.2	23.1
1986	26.5	24.3
1991	27.5	25.1

[1] Mean age at first marriage computed using Hajnal method and data from:

Statistics Canada, 1941 Census of Canada, Vol. 3, Table 7.

Statistics Canada, 1951 Census of Canada, Vol. 2, Table 2.

Statistics Canada, 1956 Census of Canada, Vol. 1, Table 28.

Statistics Canada, 1961 Census of Canada, Vol. 1, Part 3, Table 78.

Statistics Canada, 1966 Census of Canada, Vol. 1, Table 34.

Statistics Canada, *Marital Status by Age Group.* 1971 Census of Canada, Catalogue No. 92-730, Table 1.

Statistics Canada, *Marital Status by Age Group.* 1976 Census of Canada, Catalogue No. 92-825, Table 22.

Statistics Canada, *Age, Sex and Marital Status.* 1981 Census of Canada, Catalogue No. 92-901, Table 4.

Statistics Canada, *Age, Sex and Marital Status.* 1986 Census of Canada, Catalogue No. 93-101, Table 5.

Statistics Canada, *Age, Sex and Marital Status.* 1991 Census of Canada, Catalogue No. 93-310, Table 3.

Table A.5
Percentage Never-married Population (Single) by Age Group and Sex, Canada 1971-1991

Age group and sex	1971	1976	1981	1986	1991
Male					
15+	31.6	31.4	31.3	30.7	29.8
15 to 19	98.4	98.0	98.4	98.7	98.7
20 to 24	67.6	67.7	71.9	79.2	81.6
25 to 29	25.6	27.0	32.0	39.6	45.7
30 to 34	13.3	13.1	15.0	19.6	24.2
35 to 39	10.3	9.1	9.3	11.4	14.8
40 to 44	9.4	8.2	7.8	8.3	9.8
45 to 49	9.1	8.3	7.5	7.2	7.6
50 to 54	8.7	8.3	7.8	7.1	6.7
55 to 59	9.2	8.0	7.8	7.4	6.6
60+	10.3	9.2	8.2	7.5	7.0
Female					
15+	25.0	24.6	24.5	23.9	23.2
15 to 19	92.5	91.8	93.3	95.3	95.6
20 to 24	43.5	45.3	51.1	60.2	64.6
25 to 29	15.4	16.3	20.0	25.7	29.7
30 to 34	9.1	9.1	10.5	13.3	16.3
35 to 39	7.3	6.8	7.3	8.6	10.7
40 to 44	6.9	6.2	6.1	6.7	7.9
45 to 49	7.0	6.2	5.8	5.8	6.4
50 to 54	7.7	6.5	6.0	5.6	5.6
55 to 59	9.0	7.3	6.3	5.9	5.5
60+	10.5	9.8	8.9	7.9	7.2

Sources: Statistics Canada, *Marital Status by Age Group.* 1971 Census of Canada, Catalogue No. 92-730, Table 1.

Statistics Canada, *Marital Status by Age Group.* 1976 Census of Canada, Catalogue No. 92-825, Table 22.

Statistics Canada, *Age, Sex and Marital Status.* 1981 Census of Canada, Catalogue No. 92-901, Table 4.

Statistics Canada, *Age, Sex and Marital Status.* 1986 Census of Canada, Catalogue No. 93-101, Table 5.

Statistics Canada, *Age, Sex and Marital Status.* 1991 Census of Canada, Catalogue No. 93-310, Table 3.

Table A.6
Divorced Persons per 1,000 Married Persons (with spouse present) by Age Group and Sex, Canada 1971-1991

Age group and sex	1971	1976	1981	1986	1991
Male					
15+	15.7	22.4	35.3	46.0	55.1
15 to 19	27.9	11.0	12.3	30.7	33.5
20 to 24	7.2	7.8	10.3	10.6	11.2
25 to 29	12.1	17.5	25.0	23.7	24.7
30 to 34	15.5	23.7	36.0	41.9	43.6
35 to 39	17.2	26.3	41.8	54.2	62.3
40 to 44	18.3	27.5	45.8	62.3	73.4
45 to 49	18.6	28.3	46.2	63.4	77.5
50 to 54	18.2	26.7	45.0	61.3	73.5
55 to 59	17.7	24.2	39.6	55.4	66.4
60+	14.5	18.8	27.5	35.4	43.9
Female					
15+	21.5	34.7	51.9	68.8	83.3
15 to 19	7.8	5.8	5.6	10.3	11.1
20 to 24	10.1	13.7	16.8	15.4	16.0
25 to 29	19.5	30.5	40.1	39.3	36.5
30 to 34	23.6	41.5	58.3	67.7	63.2
35 to 39	24.7	45.1	69.4	88.2	92.3
40 to 44	25.0	44.9	70.8	100.0	115.4
45 to 49	24.6	42.3	67.2	94.8	124.4
50 to 54	24.1	38.7	60.7	86.1	114.4
55 to 59	24.2	34.6	53.1	75.8	103.4
60+	21.4	29.4	42.6	58.3	79.3

Calculated from:

Statistics Canada, 1971 Census of Canada, unpublished tabulations.

Statistics Canada, 1976 Census of Canada, unpublished tabulations.

Statistics Canada, 1981 Census of Canada, unpublished tabulations.

Statistics Canada, 1986 Census of Canada, unpublished tabulations.

Statistics Canada, *Age, Sex and Marital Status.* 1991 Census of Canada, Catalogue No. 93-310, Table 3.

Table A.7
Persons in Common-law Unions by Age Group and Sex, Canada 1981, 1986 and 1991

Age group		1981	1986	1991
15+	T	713,215	973,880	1,451,905
	M	356,605	486,940	725,955
	F	356,610	486,940	725,950
15 to 19	T	40,790	26,190	32,705
	M	8,340	4,655	6,570
	F	32,450	21,535	26,135
20 to 24	T	192,705	205,135	227,685
	M	83,080	81,630	89,200
	F	109,625	123,500	138,485
25 to 29	T	165,795	238,750	332,900
	M	88,120	122,670	163,840
	F	77,675	116,085	169,060
30 to 34	T	109,025	167,070	271,305
	M	61,160	90,335	140,410
	F	47,865	76,730	130,900
35 to 39	T	68,045	117,680	193,290
	M	38,715	65,010	101,310
	F	29,325	52,670	91,985
40 to 44	T	42,940	76,345	142,225
	M	24,230	42,395	76,740
	F	18,715	33,950	65,490
45 to 49	T	30,905	47,630	95,695
	M	17,630	26,525	53,570
	F	13,275	21,110	42,130
50 to 54	T	23,605	33,645	58,470
	M	13,315	19,215	34,155
	F	10,290	14,430	24,310
55 to 59	T	16,530	24,120	38,700
	M	9,080	13,710	24,020
	F	7,450	10,410	14,680

Table A.7
Persons in Common-law Unions by Age Group and Sex, Canada 1981, 1986 and 1991 (Concluded)

Age group		1981	1986	1991
60 to 65	T	10,510	16,870	26,045
	M	5,740	9,245	16,330
	F	4,770	7,625	9,715
65+	T	12,370	20,450	32,885
	M	7,200	11,555	19,820
	F	5,170	8,895	13,065

Sources: Statistics Canada, 1981 Census of Canada, unpublished tabulations.

Statistics Canada, 1986 Census of Canada, unpublished tabulations.

Statistics Canada, *Age, Sex and Marital Status.* 1991 Census of Canada, Catalogue No. 93-310, Table 6.

Table A.8
Couples in Private Households by Marital Status, Canada, Provinces and Territories, 1991

	All couples	Married couples	Common-law couples
Canada	**6,401,455**	**5,675,505**	**725,950**
Newfoundland	132,790	122,830	9,960
Prince Edward Island	29,520	27,490	2,030
Nova Scotia	211,490	191,370	20,120
New Brunswick	171,465	155,575	15,890
Quebec	1,614,350	1,307,445	306,905
Ontario	2,383,935	2,201,780	182,155
Manitoba	248,565	227,255	21,310
Saskatchewan	227,325	209,575	17,750
Alberta	584,975	525,025	59,950
British Columbia	780,285	694,655	85,630
Yukon	6,070	4,650	1,420
Northwest Territories	10,680	7,850	2,830

Source: Statistics Canada, *Families: Number, Type and Structure.* 1991 Census of Canada, Catalogue No. 93-312, Tables 5 and 6.

Table A.9
Persons Living in Common-law Unions by Age Group and Legal Marital Status, Canada, 1991

Age group	Total	Single	Separated	Divorced	Widowed
			Absolute numbers		
Total	1,451,905	923,400	102,430	376,455	49,610
15 to 19	32,705	32,460	90	135	20
20 to 24	227,685	221,995	2,330	3,205	140
25 to 29	332,900	297,050	10,200	25,010	645
30 to 34	271,305	193,255	17,315	58,980	1,745
35 to 39	193,290	94,110	19,140	76,965	3,070
40 to 44	142,225	41,850	18,075	77,875	4,430
45 to 49	95,695	18,375	13,420	58,455	5,445
50 to 54	58,470	9,145	8,425	34,845	6,045
55 to 59	38,700	5,845	5,715	20,515	6,625
60 to 64	26,045	3,970	3,735	11,590	6,745
65+	32,885	5,345	3,980	8,885	14,670
			Percentages		
Total	100.0	63.6	7.1	25.9	3.4
15 to 19	100.0	99.3	0.3	0.4	0.1
20 to 24	100.0	97.5	1.0	1.4	0.1
25 to 29	100.0	89.2	3.1	7.5	0.2
30 to 34	100.0	71.2	6.4	21.7	0.6
35 to 39	100.0	48.7	9.9	39.8	1.6
40 to 44	100.0	29.4	12.7	54.8	3.1
45 to 49	100.0	19.2	14.0	61.1	5.7
50 to 54	100.0	15.6	14.4	59.6	10.3
55 to 59	100.0	15.1	14.8	53.0	17.1
60 to 64	100.0	15.2	14.3	44.5	25.9
65+	100.0	16.3	12.1	27.0	44.6

Source: Statistics Canada, *Age, Sex and Marital Status.* 1991 Census of Canada, Catalogue No. 93-310, Table 6.